About the Author

Karel de Laat completed his bachelor's and master's degrees in psychology and his doctorate in history in Australia. He worked as an organizational psychologist for forty years, specializing in organization and career development. During this time he featured in newspapers and on radio, providing practical advice on how to achieve personal and business success, as well as presenting seminars on a wide range of business and career development subjects. In his spare time, Karel served in the Royal Australian Naval Reserve for thirty years, attaining the rank of Rear-Admiral. He now devotes his time to writing, mentoring, consulting and public speaking. His other books include *Hints for Personal Success, Business Tips, Personal Success Strategies and Career Management Strategies*.

I0169234

About the Book

Goal Achievement Strategies is a book in the Psychoframe (psychological framework) series that Karel de Laat created as part of a major organization development program for a large steel works. He had to produce a simple, practical, but powerful, supervisory management and goal achievement program that everyone in the enterprise could understand and implement on the shop floor. In addition, each part of the program had to be linked so that managers, supervisors, operators, customer service and all other support staff worked on principles that reinforced teamwork. The Goal Achievement part of the program formed the base of an interlocking structure that held the team together. Every member of the team used the same goal achievement principles to structure their work in a way that extended the base principles of plan and initiate by adding incentives for innovation, quality checking and standardization of work processes. The result was an enterprise system that provided all team members with a system for working effectively and creatively as part of an evolving team based organization. In *Goal Achievement Strategies* Karel explains how the system was developed and how you can use the same system to be more effective in achieving both your personal and career goals.

Some nursery rhymes about goal achievement[1]

Your mare is lame she halts downe right
Then shall we not get to *London* tonight:
You'd cry'd ho, ho, mony made her go
But now I well perceive it is not so
You must spur her up, and put her to't
Though money will not make her goe, your spurs will do't.

See- saw Margery Daw,
Jacky shall have a new master;
Jacky shall have but a penny a day,
Because he can't work any faster

Will you lend me your mare to ride a mile?
No, she is lame leaping over a stile.
Alack! And I must go to the fair,
I'll give you good money for lending your mare.
Oh, oh! Say you so?
Money will make the mare to go.

© Frans Karel de Laat

First published 2015

This book is copyright. Apart from any fair dealing for the purpose of private study, research or review, as permitted under the Copyright Act, no part may be reproduced by any process without written permission. This is an international edition and enquiries regarding copyright should be addressed to the publisher.

Published by:
de Laat & Co
PO Box 9 Ferny Hills Distribution Center
Brisbane QLD Australia 4055
www.delaatco.com

The preferred citation for this book is

FK de Laat, *Goal Achievement Strategies*, de Laat & Co, Brisbane, 2015.

Author: Karel de Laat
Title: *Goal Achievement Strategies*/Karel de Laat
ISBN: 978-0-9872878-3-0
Subjects: psychology, philosophy, business

Goal Achievement Strategies

How to be innovative, efficient and effective

Karel de Laat

de Laat & Co

A great deal of the joy of life consists in doing things perfectly, or at least to the best of one's ability everything which he attempts to do. There is a sense of satisfaction, a pride in surveying such a work – a work which is rounded, full, exact, complete in all its arts – which the superficial man, who leaves his work in a slovenly, slipshod, half-finished condition, can never know. It is this conscientious completeness which turns work into art. The smallest thing, well done, becomes artistic.

William Matthew

Contents

Preface

Writing about goal achievement is adding to a lot of already published material I know. So why do it? As my father used to say so often, you really know you are destined to do something when you do it because you cannot help yourself and that is exactly where I am at. I do not know how big the market is for my ideas, but I finally have the time to commit them to writing so here goes.

The defining of goals is often described as being a long way to achieving them, and so is dreaming about (or visualising) them. I am not convinced. The visualising and dreaming about process can definitely contribute to accepting the validity of your goals and assist in reducing anxiety in competition or other pressure situations, but you have to have a plan to get where you want to go.

I recall talking to a young woman who was just busting to get out there and make things happen. She had energy to burn. The only trouble was she was not sure what she wanted to burn it on. She kept trying different things and letting them drop by the wayside. To get on track this young woman's confidence and commitment needed to be directed to a worthwhile achievable goal. Sounds boring I know, but the excitement can be increased by good old fashioned planning and organising believe it or not. That is what this book is all about.

I have tried to make it more exciting by sticking closely to the theme that all the planning in the world is no use without the fire in the belly, and so on. There is no doubt that nothing will happen unless you get up and do something about what you want. Even the writers who say that you should project positive thoughts inevitably end up using for their success stories people who planned well and worked hard.

That does not mean that success is only for people who are jumping out of their skin.

One of the most successful people I ever met was a man at the other end of the spectrum from our burning to do it right now young woman. He was quiet, determined and highly successful at sales because he had a plan. He followed his plan through thick and thin and was very successful.

The mix of enthusiasm, energy good old fashioned hard work and careful planning are what makes success.

Anyway, let's get into it. I have not tried to be all things to all people, but I hope there are enough ideas to give most people something to work with.

Good luck.

Karel de Laat

You better live your best and act your best and think your best today; for today is the sure preparation for tomorrow and all the other tomorrows that follow.

Harriet Martineau

Chapter One

Introduction

Goal Achievement Strategies is the third book in the Psychoframe series. The other books are *Personal Success Strategies, Career Management Strategies, Practical Management Strategies* and *Customer Service Strategies.*

Goal Achievement Strategies is designed to assist you to clarify your goals and learn strategies for maximizing self-organization so that you can achieve those goals. As part of the process, I recommend that you learn and practice a relaxation and visualisation procedure for focusing yourself on the achievement of your goals. There are many variations on this theme and good materials are readily available both on line and in bookshops. We will include this process as part of the accompanying material to supplement concentration on the main structure of plan, initiate, innovate, check and standardise that forms the basis of the overall strategy you will learn.[2]

How it works

Goal Achievement Strategies operates on the principle that an organised method of self management by planning goals, using personal initiative, being innovative, achieving high quality by setting personal standards and implementing efficient procedures to make the work easier is the key to maximum personal efficiency. Like other Psychoframe books, *Goal Achievement Strategies* employs a program learning style and uses the Goal Achievement Questionnaire (GAQ) to measure how much you understand and are prepared to commit to principles of self-organization, motivation, innovation, quality and efficiency.

Using the information from the Goal Achievement Questionnaire, you are able to develop strategies for application in everyday situations.

As indicated earlier, for the achievement of effectiveness, *Goal Achievement Strategies* incorporates a relaxation and visualisation technique to teach you focus by rehearsing the behaviour necessary to achieve the goals that are contained in your Goal Review Form (GRF) and to acquire the skills highlighted by the Goal Achievement Questionnaire.

The goal visualisation process in combination with relaxation is not new. It has been used, particularly by a variety of sports coaches and other trainers, for many years. It is well documented in both academic and popular literature and started from the work done by Edmund Jacobsen on progressive relaxation.[3]

The relaxation and visualisation technique has been used in a variety of therapeutic settings, but its success in these areas seems to be much less predictable than its application in situations where a person is trying to improve a particular skill or behaviour.

Nevertheless, the use of such techniques should always be kept in context as aids to learning and general performance, which is how they are used in *Goal Achievement Strategies.* If you find they are useful with the limited information available in the book, then keep using them.

My real hope is that the exploration of such techniques and the general concept of values development and behaviour shaping will encourage you to read more widely in philosophy and psychology for both enjoyment and personal development.

Every book is just a speck in the amount of knowledge available to you and should lead you to consider the many ideas that can broaden your goals and your life experience. The techniques that follow are no exception. Use them critically and I hope you search out other learning experience as a result of what you learn about yourself. In the next section, I provide an overview of the program and its aims.

Overview

We are all learning all the time. Unfortunately, what we learn may not be the best material to make us happy or help us to achieve what we want from life. One of the most basic principles of the techniques recommended as part of *Goal Achievement Strategies* is that you think more about what you hear, see and feel and how it influences your life experience.

Complementing this initial principle of being more alert to the influences of your environment is the principle that you can shape psychological frameworks (Psychoframes), composed of your preferred view of the world, to help you be more confident and achieve what you want in managing these external influences.

In this regard, what *Goal Achievement Strategies* provides is a skills training process in which an assessment is done of personal goals and personal skills before the program commences. In a simple process, a Goal Review Form (GRF) is used to allow you to record your goals at the beginning of the process, which you keep and use for future planning.

As an important part of the process, a Goal Achievement Questionnaire (GAQ) is used that allows you to learn about your current levels of skill and then becomes the basis upon which your training is conducted and your skills are developed.

It is natural to be nervous about things that are new, challenge your current beliefs and that use any form of assessment. This process does all of these things. For this reason, the process is self administering, self marking and self analysed to put you in charge of the process and give you confidence right from the start.

The documents are very personal and not intended to be compared to anyone else's results. They are merely used as a guide to help you get the best results using the process.

After the Goal Review Form has been completed, and before doing the Goal Achievement Questionnaire, it is important to re-consider what you want to achieve and if the answers you provided to any of the questions indicate that this is not the right process to be undertaking at this time. It could be that you need to be doing more work on positive thinking and confidence using *Personal Success Strategies* before undertaking the goal achievement process. [1] You may be more vocationally focused, for example, and *Career Management Strategies* may better suit your needs.[2]

Considerations like those above are designed to keep the process of you personal development firmly in your grasp. The learning paradigm is about being self directed in what you want and how you get there. All the options you pursue should be about fully informed learning and not slavish copying of what others have found useful.

In using the Goal Review Form it is very important to review your life history and identify areas that are of greatest importance to you and which will thus become the focus of your major achievements. The rule that 10% or 20% of *Goal Achievement Strategies* process and content will account for about 80% or 90% of your feeling of achievement is normally a good way to keep the self directed and selective nature of the process clear in your mind.

At all times, you should be looking for those areas where most effort should be concentrated. This is a principle you need to 'internalize' at the earliest possible time to assist you to get focussed on the areas that will be most important to you. The five basic *Goal Achievement Strategies* of Planning, Initiating, Innovating, Checking and Standardising will be explained to you in detail with many examples. Within this psychological framework, personal examples from your life are important to develop confidence in how you are managing the information and how you intend to relate it to you innermost thoughts and desires.

---

[1] Karel de Laat, *Personal Success Strategies,* de Laat & Co, Brisbane, 2015.
[2] Karel de Laat, *Career Management Strategies*, de Laat & Co, Brisbane, 2015.

Without in any way reducing the impact of the long term us of the strategies, it is important to understand that the process of change begins immediately. From the time that you start considering how far you have progressed with your goals, learning new behaviours is something that will be on your mind immediately. As soon as you progress to your first Personal Action List for Plan, Initiate, Innovate, Check or Standardize one of your most important goal achievement processes you will be working on new behaviours.

On an ongoing basis you will be listing key words, actions and events that will form the basis of your new ways of behaving that you can focus on and reinforce. You will do this in various forms of relaxation, visualisation or any form of motivational technique that you found most helpful as part of *Personal Success Strategies* or any other process you find helpful.[4]

Most importantly, as with any habit or skill, practice by repetition is critical to acquisition of any new skills and behaviours.[5] You will have little likelihood of any success without committing to making these new techniques a routine part of your daily life. Use of visualisation, for example, should be repeated throughout the day and applied to all your goals.

Keep in mind, however, that visualization does not make the goal magically appear it is a technique to keep you focused and improve the attention, anticipation and concentration that brings success. The learning is about living a mindful active life where the processes are intertwined into your real goals. Visualization, for example, is not about living a dream life.

As you progress through the various chapters that discuss the *Goal Achievement Strategies* you will see that your responses to the Goal Achievement Questionnaire form part of a new process for more formally considering how you go about achieving what you want. More formal repeat self assessments using the Goal Review Form and developing a Goal Achievement Profile from the Goal Achievement Questionnaire can be used if you wish.

Such assessments can be useful, but investigating your current and future behaviours as you set them out in the Personal Action List is a powerful way to clarify how you plan to incorporate planning, initiating, innovating, checking and standardising into your goal directed behaviour.

This is also the point at which you will be able to start developing an awareness of your level of commitment. You will be able to assess this from the types of goals that you set and how much effort you are prepared to put into the process. Commitment to clear and simple goals is an essential part of success with any process but in pursuit of life goals it is the key.

Whatever your level of commitment, it is essential that you commit some time to your development on a daily basis, work hard to understand the principles of the process and develop your overall personal knowledge of success strategies. Only in this way can you participate in and then drive the things that will help you achieve your goals.

The regular use of relaxation and visualisation can be helpful, if that works for you, but the capacity to use the material in this book and the associated techniques varies widely. While some people experience immediate results others find it more difficult. This has to be managed by you as part of your self-development strategy.

You may find that simple awareness and use of the *Goal Achievement Strategies* of planning, initiating, innovating, checking and standardising and being systematic gives you much greater rewards than just using the relaxation and visualisation material. You need to work with what works for you. Do not think it needs to be complicated. The simple ways, if they work, are the best, in everything.

The goals to be achieved rely on a clear understanding by you of the principles of the process and a commitment to doing the work necessary to get the results either in development of behaviours using the *Goal Achievement Strategies* and/or relaxation and visualisation techniques.

As you progress through the process you will find that you can begin to fine tune Goal Achievement behaviours. New goals can be set as you make progress with the original goals but the focus from the Goal Review Forms and the Personal Action Lists (PAL) completed each week must be maintained. An important part of the process is widening your view and your learning experiences to include more material that you access independently and the sharing of your new knowledge and skills with ***similarly minded and supportive people***. Bringing mental rehearsal to life in discussions and 'role plays' with others is a key part of socialising the new you, but choose your new colleagues carefully.

Discussions and role plays should be rewarding for both people and you should compare the success of these rehearsals with the rehearsals in your mind of the key behaviours needed to achieve your goals. In addition, as you progress with *Goal Achievement Strategies*, more written work may be appropriate such as completion of time management activities as part of planning, use of creative thinking exercises or reference to lateral thinking texts for innovation. This will depend on your goals as well as your previous experience.

As you progress it will become more important to reinforce your understanding of the principles. In particular you will need to remain aware that long term goal achievement through constant self-management and using the techniques of planning, initiating, innovating, checking and standardising, is a new set of skills. You must remain aware that this process is not a short term solution that finishes when you get to the end of this book. It is a learning and skills acquisition process that is designed to give long term benefits because of long term behaviour change. With regard to behaviour change, you should start to see real progress in your thinking and behaviour modification in at least some areas and it is important to compare where you are making most and least progress. Those areas where most progress has been made should be analysed so that you can repeat the success behaviour using the *Goal Achievement Strategies* technique and/or relaxation and visualisation processes.

Areas where least progress has been made should be analysed so that new behaviours can be rehearsed and specific behavioural goals can be set for these areas. These variations in development will become clearer whenever the Goal Achievement Questionnaire is re-administered. At these times, it is also important to consider the link between the Goal Achievement Questionnaire (GAQ) and your actual behaviour in thinking and acting on a day to day basis.

The final stage of the process will occur when you are reviewing your behavioural goals regularly and/or conducting relaxation and visualisation sessions on a daily basis. At this stage, you should be taking 'the lead' by using the material to work on specific goals that you develop as you gain confidence.

At this point, the Goal Review Form (GRF) can be completed again with the view that this will provide your long term goal focus. The process of using the GRF and the GAQ and comparing your results is meant to be a transparent look at your progress not a comparison of 'tests'. It can help to think of it in the same way as improvement in a physical fitness training program except the training is mental.

As you conclude the process for the first time, you need to resist completely the temptation to go over old ground and re-open old issues. Your focus should be entirely on confirming achievements and re-iterating the *Goal Achievement Strategies* that you now have in place. In doing this you need to affirm the benefits of long term use of relaxation and visualisation techniques and the application of the *Goal Achievement Strategies* in conducting your day to day activities.

In every phase where you re-do the GRF and GAQ you should conclude with a firm written statement of the goals to be achieved and a firm statement by you in relation to your commitment to the achievement of those goals. This provides you with a personal record of your progress that you can use to look back and see how far you have come.

Some theory about the goal achievement process

In this section of the introduction I will explain in a more formal way how *Goal Achievement Strategies* is structured to achieve a learning outcome. I will try to keep it 'tight' and relevant, but there will still be some 'dry' material, so please stick with me on this as the more formal guidelines that follow are my way of standardising what I am doing in this book and creating a formal framework for self learning..

The *Goal Achievement Strategies* Process

The purpose of the process in the book is to provide competency based training to develop skills in planning, initiating, innovating, checking and standardising for individuals to effectively achieve their pre-defined goals.

The Target Audience

The process is suitable for participants who have at least a minimal understanding of personal and work related goal achievement. It is also suitable for participants who have extensive work experience and are seeking a model to apply for personal or work related effectiveness.

On successful completion of the learning process, you should be able to:

- Plan work activities to meet specific objectives.
- Initiate work activities or individual goal achievement using the best processes available.
- Be innovative in the application of your skills to personal or work related goals.
- Implement personal quality management strategies.
- Develop and implement standard systems for maximising personal efficiency and effectiveness.

The process assumes certain competencies such as you being able to read and write and maintain an effective relationship with fellow students and colleagues. Nevertheless, the process can still be implemented by a tutor in such a way that limitations in literacy and communication skills are overcome. In these cases, the need to confirm understanding becomes much more important and expectations of self management need to be reviewed.

In addition, there is a preference that you

- Be committed to improving your personal efficiency and effectiveness.
- Display an appreciation of the need for structured approaches to goal achievement.
- Be motivated towards personal independence and self guided decision making.

Nominal Time Allocation

The process described in this book can be delivered through classroom or tutorial based instruction as well as self study. In these cases, a nominal class time of six contact hours is recommended for participants with the preferred entry competencies. Two additional hours are required for assessment. This time allocation should be adjusted for alternative learning modes.

Assessment Principles

The methods by which evidence of achievement of competence is assessed must be specific and clearly understood by participants.

The demands of any assessment should be no more than is required to demonstrate competency. Demonstration requires assessment of the task or project during performance as well as evaluation of the finished product.

The method(s) chosen should be appropriate to the information sought in the environment in which assessments may be logically, safely and economically conducted.

The real focus of *Goal Achievement Strategies* is on the learning outcomes that follow. They are action based and should be openly discussed at all times.

Learning Outcome One

Plan work activities to meet specific objectives

Performance Criteria:

1.1   An action priority schedule listing specific personal objectives is developed.

1.2   Specific objectives are analysed using priority planning and time management principles.

1.3   A completed plan of work activities to meet specific objectives is presented to the facilitator and/or critically analysed by the participant.

Assessment

The participant will demonstrate competency by achieving an above average score on the Planning dimension on the Goal Achievement Questionnaire.

Competency will be demonstrated by development of a written plan, presenting the ideas from the written plan verbally and giving a critique of both the written plan and the presentation.

Learning Outcome Two

Initiate work activities or individual goal achievement plans using the best processes available.

Performance Criteria:

2.1   Principles for developing initiatives for the achievement of personal goals are listed on the Goal Achievement Action Priorities schedule.

2.2   The desired behaviours are presented to the facilitator verbally or self analysed.

2.3   The written plan and/or a verbal presentation are critiqued by the participant and/or discussed with the facilitator.

Assessment

The participant will demonstrate competency by achieving an above average score on the Initiating dimension on the Goal Achievement Questionnaire. Competency will be demonstrated by developing a written plan, presenting the ideas from the written plan verbally and giving a critique of both the written plan and the presentation.

Learning Outcome Three

Be innovative in the application of skills to personal or work related goals

Performance Criteria

3.1   Practical innovative strategies to be implemented by the participant are listed on the Goal Achievement Action Priorities Schedule.

3.2 The participant demonstrates the application of innovation by reporting/recording appropriate behaviours implemented in a real life setting assessment.

Assessment

The participant will demonstrate competency by obtaining an above average score on the innovation dimension of the Goal Achievement Questionnaire. Competency will be demonstrated by recounting/recording incidents of innovation in Goal Achievement from real life experience.

Learning Outcome Four

Implement personal quality management strategies

Performance Criteria:

4.1 Strategies appropriate for introducing quality management into the day to day activities of the participant are listed on the Goal Achievement Action Priority Schedule.

4.2 The participant explains the implementation of personal quality management systems from real life experience and critiques the benefits independently or with the facilitator.

Assessment _

The participant will demonstrate competency by performing at an above average level on the checking dimension of the Goal Achievement Questionnaire. Competency will also be demonstrated by recounting/recording personal quality management behaviour from real life.

Learning Outcome Five

Develop standard systems to improve efficiency

Performance Criteria:

5.1   The participant will list strategies for improving efficiency in personal performance by development of standard systems of Goal Achievement.

5.2   The participant will analyse personal performance strategies using standardised systems of development thinking and critique the quality of the process independently or with the facilitator.

Assessment

The participant will demonstrate competency by performing at an above average level on the standardising dimension of the Goal Achievement Questionnaire. Competency will be demonstrated by developing standard systems for Goal Achievement in real life and critiquing these independently or with the facilitator.

Relevant Work Conditions:

The relevant work context for demonstration of competence is the:

- participant's immediate personal goal achievement environment or work setting.
- typical environment and task responsibilities.
- network of other individuals or groups that are influenced by the outcomes.

Participants will be expected to meet:

- Task deadlines.
- Quality standards.
- Other mutually agreed performance parameters.

Content

It is intended that topics on the content list be dealt with only at the level required by the learning outcomes and performance criteria. In some cases it may entail only a reference to them and not a detailed study.

In designing the learning program to support learning outcomes, content should include the recommended over lapping areas of knowledge, skills and attributes.

Learning outcomes are to be achieved through structured, interactive and participative learning activities based on the following topics:

- Knowledge

- Planning Processes

- Initiating Behaviour

- Innovative Strategies

- Checking and Quality Management

- Standardised Systems of Goal Achievement

Skills

- Work Planning

- Prioritisation

- Time Management

- Note Taking Summarising

- Decision Making and Problem Solving

- Giving and Receiving Feedback

- Questioning

Attributes

- Committed

- Open Minded

- Flexible

- Motivated

- Creative

- Initiating

- Detail Minded

- Quality Minded

Principles of Delivery

The *Goal Achievement Strategies* process aims to develop the personal effectiveness skills of participants with individual or shared responsibility for work. It draws upon the individuals' personal goal achievement and/or workplace goal achievement experiences. All activities should not only reflect the desired learning outcomes and performance criteria, but should be relevant to the participant.

The learning process is designed for delivery, individually or in groups, in the classroom, or in a variety of modes including self study, teleconferencing and interactive video. It is vital, however, that the process be experienced in a way that will suit the participants and any organizations involved. Case studies, activities, materials and general delivery methods must fit the industry/work and participant context. The teaching and learning methods may well vary with each participant, individual or group, the needs of which will be reflected in the activities undertaken. These will still match learning outcomes and performance criteria.

The participants must be actively involved in, and communicated with, in regard to what is to be covered and how they are to achieve the aims of *Goal Achievement Strategies*. If there is a facilitator this person should adopt a participant centred and facilitative role in employing the skills and experience of all participants and focusing on issues relevant to the social context of each participant.

The facilitator should select a range of strategies that integrate theory and practice. These strategies should include case studies, group discussions where appropriate, practical exercises, role plays, simulations, and other action or experiential learning activities which will enable participants to examine and monitor their existing and newly developed skills, knowledge and attributes. Some areas of content are common to more than one learning outcome. These should be integrated throughout the process.

Conclusion

Ultimately, the success of any process rests with the individual participant. If the contents of *Goal Achievement Strategies* meet your needs at this point in time, then you are more likely to use the concepts involved. Alternatively, the strategies may be used as an adjunct to a wider development plan.

Whether you are using *Goal Achievement Strategies* as a single process or in conjunction with other books in the Personal Success series, it is important to place any activity in context by doing other research.

The material contained in the following chapters is just one approach to achieving what you want out of life. A key concept in this and all the Personal Success books is that uncritical acceptance of any learning is a contradiction in terms. Learning means listening, understanding, evaluating, comparing, testing, applying and then further evaluating ideas as you gain more experience.

Please think about what is said in this book and elsewhere on the basis that it is information that you can use, but only you can makes decisions about what your goals are, how much you want to invest in achieving them and deciding when you are content that you have done all that you can do to achieve what you want out of life.

The reproduction of the more formal aspects of the original coaching syllabus is not usual in the personal success books but the Goal Achievement Strategies approach has more comparative content than both Personal Success Strategies and Career Management Strategies.

The context is also more competitive in that you are likely to experience in other more self focused development activities. Your goal should be to keep the competitive aspects as a motivational guide not as odious comparisons.

Chapter Two

Reviewing Your Goals

Introduction to the Goal Review Form (GRF).

The Goal Review Form (GRF) lets you define what it is that you want. So many of us think we know what it is we are after in life, but somehow until we put it in writing there does not seem to be any focus or direction established.

This is your permanent record of what you want today. You keep it! You manage it! You decide if you are going to do anything about it!

Shortly you will complete the Goal Achievement Questionnaire (GAQ) and find out if you have the tools and attitude to make real progress toward your goals.

Remember, goals are what you want them to be. They can be personal or business, private or public, physical or spiritual. Just fill in the words that mean the most to you.

The GRF is a tool. It is included again at the end of the book so that you can copy it and fill it out as many times as you like as your goals change and develop.

This is just the beginning. As you gain more experience of how to use the concepts in *Goal Achievement Strategies* you can develop your approach using your own ideas as well as ideas from other sources. Some people find it helpful to keep all their work in a hard copy folder, others prefer to display the material in their private environment and others prefer to have it on their computer tablet or mobile phone. Whatever works for you is the best option.

Goal Review Form (GRF)

Name: _____

Date: _____

1.   Currently, success to me means

_____

_____

_____

2.   Rate where are you now with respect to this current goal by marking an X along the Scale of Success to indicate your current progress.

Scale of Success

0   20   40   60   80   100%
Just Starting   Where I want to be

3.   Strategies for the achievement of my success goals

ACTION   BY WHEN

_____

_____

_____

_____

_____

_____

Chapter Three

Goal Achievement Strategies

Introduction to the Goal Achievement Questionnaire (GAQ)

The personal success series is a learning program based on getting you committed to using a structured approach to achieving your goals and the GAQ is an essential part of getting that to happen.

Our attitudes are formed by how we react to new situations. How we do that is not always in the way we would like if we really thought about it. Using tools like the GAQ you get to go back over situations where you had some attitudes formed, in this case relating to goal achievement, and take more time working out how you would prefer to do it rather than just reacting on the spot.

Imagine the earliest time of having to do your domestic chores at home or doing your schoolwork. For most of us, we did not get on with it immediately, we usually waited till someone else came along and made us start or we waited till the last minute. Then we rushed and made a bad job of it and started a cycle that repeated itself time and again. The habit of procrastination was born and soon spread itself into a range of other areas.

With the GAQ, you get to look at the behaviors you have developed, think again about how you would like them to be and begin defining a new approach. You compare your efforts against the perfect response (of course there is no perfect response, but I have tried to think up some good ones) and decide on a learning strategy.

As with the GRF, you get to fill out the GAQ as many times as you like and as often as you like. The GAQ is not an exam. It is part of the learning process where you get to shape attitudes which help you achieve what you want.

There are all sorts of little psychological games going on in your mind at the same time that help you as well. For example, the more time you voluntarily put into the program the more your brain tells you it has to be worthwhile and the more you start to take on the new attitudes to compensate. Our brain has this amazing need to rationalise our behaviour, but so often it works against us. With *Goal Achievement Strategies*, you make it work for you.

Most of all it is best to let your head go with the responses. You don't have to say a lot, but try to get as many one word ideas down as you can. The detailed instructions show you how it works. See you on the other side of the experience.

Please turn over and start the questionnaire

GOAL ACHIEVEMENT QUESTIONNAIRE (GAQ)

Name: _____ Date:_____

INSTRUCTIONS

The Goal Achievement Questionnaire (GAQ) is designed to help you learn more about your approach to managing personal challenges. It is open-ended and requires written answers.

The questionnaire contains a series of statements followed by a space for you to write your response. You are required to respond as if you were speaking to someone who may make a statement or ask a question. Your response should be about your own attitudes, beliefs and experiences. You should not respond with a question.

Do not worry if you have no experience in this area. The questionnaire uses no special jargon or other expressions which would be unfamiliar to you. Alternatively, although the questions are intended to be general, you may feel happier answering in relation to a particular situation you have experienced. Feel free to use any method of approach. The aim is to allow you to give your views on a variety of issues by simulating a discussion.

HERE IS A SAMPLE OF WHAT YOU WILL BE REQUIRED TO DO

Statement: Can Goal Achievement be learned?

Response: Of course, it is a skill.

You may write as much as you like in the space provided, but you need to make only two different points to complete the item and achieve the maximum score.

The questionnaire is completed with a time limit because the situations which are simulated are usually done under pressure with no opportunity to correct errors made.

You will have 30 minutes to do as many of the questions as possible. Work quickly but not so fast that you make mistakes. Ask any questions before you begin.

PLEASE TURN OVER AND START WORK

GOAL ACHIEVEMENT QUESTIONNAIRE

1. Statement: What is the value of personal goal setting?

    Response:

    _____

    _____

2. Statement: What does it mean to be a self-starter?

    Response:

    _____

    _____

3. Statement: How can everybody be innovative?

    Response:

    _____

    _____

4. Statement: How do I know if I have done a quality job?

    Response:

    _____

    _____

5. Statement: What is personal efficiency?

    Response:

    _____

    _____

    _____

6.   Statement: How do I use goal setting to motivate myself?

        Response:

---

7.   Statement: Shouldn't I wait for someone else to show me the way?

        Response:

---

8.   Statement: Why should I always look for a better way of doing things?

        Response:

---

9.   Statement: Getting it right the first time seems pretty unrealistic to me.
        Response:

---

10.   Statement: Developing systems just seems to slow things down.
        Response:

---

11.   Statement: What is the value of planning?

        Response:

_____

_____

12.   Statement: Won't people be threatened by me taking the initiative?

        Response:

_____

_____

13.   Statement: All the best ways of doing things should have been thought of already.

        Response:

_____

_____

14.   Statement: Everybody makes mistakes!

        Response:

_____

_____

15.   Statement: What is the value of developing standard work systems?

        Response:

_____

_____

16. Statement: I could be getting things done with the time that I would waste planning.

   Response:

_____

_____

17. Statement: I just can't seem to get started on things.

   Response:

_____

_____

18. Statement: How do I innovate?

   Response:

_____

_____

19. Statement: Isn't it better to have someone else check what you do?

   Response:

_____

_____

20. Statement: What is personal effectiveness?

   Response:

_____

_____

21.　　Statement:　　How far ahead should I plan?

　　　　Response:

_____

_____

22.　　Statement:　　What's the value of having initiative?

　　　　Response:

_____

_____

23.　　Statement:　　Won't people be threatened by me always trying to find a better way?

　　　　Response:

_____

_____

24.　　Statement:　　I can't always get it right.

　　　　Response:

_____

_____

25.　　I'm just not the type of person who gets organised!

　　　　Response:

_____

_____

CHECK YOUR ANSWERS IF YOU HAVE TIME

GOAL ACHIEVEMENT ANSWERS

As I said before you completed the questionnaire, I have outlined some basic answers to illustrate the point of the GAQ. You will soon get into the swing of things as you go back over what you have written and give yourself marks.

Don't be too hard on yourself this time around. The main aim is to get you thinking about the system and how the stimulus response situation can work for you in changing how you approach the situations. You don't have to have the exact words I have used as it is the theme that is important. Just look at the words and what feeling and attitude they represent and mark accordingly. Have fun.

1.   What is the value of personal goal setting?
   o   Motivation
   o   Clarity of purpose
   o   Allows assessment

2.   What does it mean to be a self-starter?
   o   To not need others' supervision
   o   Have energy/drive/motivation
   o   Have self-confidence

3.   How can everybody be innovative?
   o   Changing for the better
   o   Using creative thinking
   o   Looking for continual improvements
   o   Be inventive/imaginative
   o   By looking forward

4.   How do I know if I have done a quality job?
   o   Meets the standards
   o   Product is functional

5. What is personal efficiency?

    o   Using the least resources required for a good job
    o   Getting the optimal result by organising materials

6. How do I use goal setting to motivate myself?

    o   Think of achievement/satisfaction on completion
    o   Set realistic goals
    o   Set a goal you desire and work towards it.

7. Shouldn't I wait for someone else to show me the way?

    o   No
    o   Increased drive if own plan
    o   Self determination of plan

8. Why should I always look for a better way of doing things.

    o   Efficiency
    o   Continous improvement is possible

9. Getting it right the first time seems pretty unrealistic to me.

    o   No
    o   Not if you check your work

10. Developing systems just seems to slow things down.

    o   No
    o   Actually working to a plan is quicker

11. What is the value of planning?

    o   Best allocation of resources
    o   Strategy for implementation

12.   Won't people be threatened by me taking the initiative?

- o   Something you do for you
- o   Self development
- o   Allow consideration

13.   All the best ways of doing things should have been thought of already.

- o   No
- o   Individuality
- o   Improvements/advancements

14.   Everybody makes mistakes!

- o   Probably yes
- o   Learning occurs
- o   Grow from experiences

15.   What is the value of developing standard work systems?

- o   Allows delegation
- o   Develops efficiency
- o   You can work to a plan

16.   I could be getting things done with the time that I would waste planning.

- o   Expression of disagreement
- o   Statement regarding value of planning

17.   I just can't seem to get started on things.

- o   Just do it
- o   Find something to motivate you
- o   With practice it will become easier

18.   How do I innovate?

- o Look for improvements
- o Use goals/brainstorming or planning
- o Be creative

19.   Isn't it better to have someone else check what you do?

- o No
- o Efficiency
- o Increases self worth or self confidence

20.   What is personal effectiveness?

- o Successful completion
- o Personally being able to do a task
- o Always having a systematic or smart approach

21.   How far ahead should I plan?

- o As necessary for achievement
- o For meaningful length of time
- o To suit your own needs

22.   What's the value of having initiative?

- o Motivation
- o Success
- o Feeling of achievement

23.   Won't people be threatened by me always trying to find a better way?

- o It's for self-development
- o Something done for you
- o People will identify it as initiative and come to expect it of you

24.   I can't always get it right.

   o Practice
   o Learn from mistakes
   o Check work

25.   I'm just not the type of person who gets organised!

   o Practice
   o Organization is a learned skill
   o You can be what you want
   o Do a little bit at a time

Developing Your Profile

If you thought that bit was fun, wait until you get into the profiling process. You may have noticed that the themes of the questions repeat themselves. I am not really that subtle I know. Anyway, the items follow the pattern five times in the same order. This is not very good if you are using a serious psychological test, but very useful for the cooperative development of a learning process.

In the next section, I will explain the principles of *Goal Achievement Strategies* and the GAQ, but for now I want you to transcribe your item scores onto the matrix below.

Remember this is a learning exercise not an exam, so think about how you are marking yourself. Be as lenient or demanding as you want to be. The whole process is about you managing the training on your own terms so the difference between the process and outcomes becomes a bit arbitrary. As I said earlier, the whole process is very transparent and that is the way it is supposed to be. The goal is to make your behaviour transparent to you and this starts with the GAQ.

If you still find it a bit of a challenge to do the marking now, go on and read the following chapters and come back.

Goal Achievement Marking Sheet

Basically, you get a point for each positive idea you wrote down about why Planning, Initiating, Innovating, Checking and Standardising lead to goal achievement. For every point you give yourself, you put a cross (starting at the bottom and working up) under Plan for points on items 1,6,11,16,21 and so on as illustrated for all skills on the Goal Achievement Profile Sheet below.

Goal Achievement Profile Sheet

Plan (Questions 1,6,11, 16 & 21)	Initiate (Questions 2,7,12,17 & 22)	Innovate (Questions 3,8,13, 18 & 23)	Check (Questions 4,9,14,19 & 24)	Standardise Questions 5,10,15, 20 & 25)
X		X	X	
X	X	X	X	X
X	X	X	X	X
X	X	X	X	X

If you add up the scores on the items and transfer the results to the columns on the profile sheet by placing a cross in a cell for each correct response you will see the results of your work displayed on a simple graph. In the next section, I explain what it means after discussing the principles underlying *Goal Achievement Strategies.*

Personal Notes on my Goal Achievement Profile

It is always useful to keep your personal commitment to any program of learning focused by describing it in your own words and from your own experiences. Having done your profile, it is a good time to reflect on your goal achievement efforts so far in your life and what the GAQ had added to your knowledge about yourself, before I talk about the wider principles behind the program and give examples of how to implement change.

No lines this time as you may be drawing pictures or diagrams as well as writing words.

Personal Reflections on Goal achievemen

Chapter Four

Key Issues

Introduction to the Basic Principles

Every idea has more to it than what is simply stated and *Goal Achievement Strategies* is no exception. I will try to keep the psychological mumbo jumbo to a minimum and just work with the things that are necessary to make sure you are in charge of the process.

Every time I conduct a goal achievement self-development training session, I get people to tell me what it is about their life that they have control over and could improve. I always hear the same things and most of them relate to motivation. Mostly, the people in the group have decided that they have control, but it is just too hard to change old habits.

Examples of how hard this is are found every day in our eating habits, lack of exercise and the list goes on. What happens when someone changes those habits is what is contained in *Goal Achievement Strategies*. They simply decide enough is enough, set a goal and go and get it.

Only you know what you want and *Goal Achievement Strategies* does not focus on one area, it lets you do that. What it does do is highlight the things that are within your power to get you to where you want to be and then let's you repeat the process as often as you like.

Sayings like 'Plan the work and work the plan' and 'Those who fail to plan, plan to fail' are so well known because they are so true. What the *Goal Achievement Strategies* does is bring these sayings to life by letting you internalize the principles using the GAQ. However, you still need to understand the principles you are using to be in charge of the process.

The principles that follow here are simple, often well known, but only effective if you use them. So let's look at what we are using.

GOAL ACHIEVEMENT STRATEGIES Basic Principles

- Plan your approach with a strategy based on systematic pursuit of goals.

- Initiate your goal achievement activities independently.

- Innovate to identify strategies to maximise effectiveness.

- Check your own performance to achieve quality.

- Standardise your methods to maximise efficiency.

These are the basic principles that *Goal Achievement Strategies* aims to have you make a commitment to remembering, using and then living by. In addition, there are action reminders to make the principles more actionable (no such word of course but it sounds good).

GOAL ACHIEVEMENT STRATEGIES Action Reminders

- Plan to achieve specific measurable goals.
- Take action on your preferred strategy immediately.
- Innovate to succeed.
- Adopt 'right first time'' as your ideal.
- Use the best system to get the best result.

In addition, there is an action plan to reinforce the day to day things you have to do to achieve your goals.

GOAL ACHIEVEMENT STRATEGIES Action Plan

PLAN

- Set realistic goals clearly and confidently.
- Plan your activities and be prepared.
- Stick to the plan.
- Review your progress against the plan.

INITIATE

- Begin at the beginning.
- Organise yourself.
- Allocate and apply selected resources.
- Look for immediate rewards.

INNOVATE

- Always look for a better way.
- Disassemble and reassemble the task/activity/process.
- Relax and visualise.
- Focus on the outcome.

CHECK

- Accept responsibility.
- Do the extra work.
- Know and apply the standard.
- Own the end result.

STANDARDISE

- Copy the best.
- Speed it up, shorten it, organise it better.
- Document the best system.
- Be the best.

As has been said by so many people so eloquently in so many ways, nothing actually happens until someone does something. Now it is up to you to list what you would do, if you had the motivation, on your **Personal Action List (PAL).**

You PAL has to include all the key words, actions & events to memorize, visualize and discuss that make your plan for goal achievement come to life. If you want to you can make some quick notes now, but the PAL is repeated again, and again, at the end of every chapter where I discuss the key behavioural areas.

Personal Action List (PAL)

Name: _____ **Date:**_____

Plan

_____

_____

_____

Initiate

_____

_____

_____

Innovate

_____

_____

_____

Check

_____

_____

_____

Standardise

_____

_____

_____

Chapter Five

Plan

Introduction

Now I know exactly what you are going to say - booooooring. Why do I know, because I feel exactly the same and this is one of my own biggest problem areas that I have to spend most of my time on to stay on track and I don't always stay on track either. Nobody's perfect, but the trouble is we too often use the saying as an excuse for giving up instead of getting motivated to achieve what we want.

Applying the Principles

If you are going to plan your approach with a strategy based on systematic pursuit of goals then you have to accept that part of your life plan is going to be about predictability. I do not intend to beat you over the head with all the examples of how people who planned to go nowhere ended up there, which would be boring.

What I want you to think about is a thing I call the 'layers of life', which I have written about elsewhere but feel cannot be over emphasized in goal achievement planning and looking at life's goals

HOW FAR DO YOU WANT TO GO?

Having spent my life assessing other people and attempting to help them realise their potential, one of the things that is most important to me is that people understand that the rewards they feel are adjusted according to the circumstances that they are in. Simply put, it is just as easy for an individual living a 'normal' life to feel pain and pleasure at the same level as individuals that may appear to be in much more privileged circumstances.

I call this phenomenon the 'layers of life'. The layers of life principle is extremely important when you consider your personal rewards and how they will affect you permanently or temporarily. If we equate those layers arbitrarily with income (and I say arbitrarily because I do not want to equate success with money alone), the lower to middle layer represents most of us, ebbing and flowing between an upper and lower level in terms of our ability to meet our financial commitments.

We spend a bit too much, we save a little bit, we save a little bit and then we spend too much, and so on. Throughout our lives, most of us are slowly rising through several layers to the point where we eventually retire and probably then drop back a layer or two in terms of the amount of money we have available to spend. This particular pattern of rising through the various layers of life is fairly common and many parts of our society are built on the assumption that this is how people will behave.

Now in terms of being successful and deciding just how you want to live your life and what you want to achieve, it is very important to realise that problems occur when someone rises too rapidly through the layers. What happens is that they are not able to accept the adjustments that go with having very little money one day to having a relatively large amount suddenly over months, sometimes days in the case of people who come upon a large amount of money through winning the lottery or something similar. They find that they cannot adjust to going from a very low band to a very high band, where last week they could spend only a limited amount of money and now suddenly their ability to spend seems unlimited.

I must emphasize that I have only used a money example as a base. Other examples can be given in terms of power, adulation and numerous other human factors which are important to our day to day satisfaction. One of the very important principles of being successful is really understanding just how far up in the various layers of life you want to eventually find yourself; and then **deciding how much effort you are prepared to put in to get where you want to go.**

We all hear stories about people who wear their money and their power ungraciously but I am going to concentrate on talking about inward directed feelings that affect you rather than the outward symptoms of overexposure to success or failure.

On various public training programs that I have conducted, I have had the opportunity to ask people to publicly declare just how ambitious they really are and it has always surprised me just how many of these people are really not that ambitious.

These examples indicate to me that most of the people who read this book will have only limited ambition and I should make it clear that being successful does not necessarily mean building your ambition levels. It means deciding the right ambition level for you and then accepting the rewards that go with that level and accepting that the effort that you put in to achieve your goals is an integral part of being successful.

Actually, an examination of the definition of ambition will give some clue as to why many people are hesitant about pursuing the upper levels of life. Most definitions of ambition show that it clearly means standing outside the group and, not surprisingly, most of us just do not want to stand out and thus be outside the group. Many of us just do not want to be outstanding.

Do not let other people decide what you are going to do. An important part of being successful is being able to

decide that you want to stay with a job or activity, which you do well and enjoy and ensure that you are recognised for the contribution that you make.

To achieve this you need to stand by your beliefs and be respected for being honest with yourself and others and about expressing how you really feel.

For example, one of my own staff was required to recruit a new executive for a client company and despite writing a quite restrictive and demanding advertisement he received in excess of 100 applications. He seemed concerned and I queried the reason. He said that in speaking to the candidates, he found that many of them were in good positions now and were unable to say why they were seeking a change other than for the money or just for the sake of a change. This lack of a comprehensive assessment of a change strategy was quite foreign to my successful team member because he had always based a move on a thorough analysis of dissatisfaction with one job or extreme attraction to another.

This is just one of many examples of how planning can fall by the wayside. Let us consider how planning fits into various types of goal achievement challenges so that you can compare and consider how you want to proceed.

Persistence and planning - it pays

I was speaking to a senior manager in one of my client groups in regard to their very well advanced and very successful management implementation system. This group is very profitable and is enjoying great success even during the current economic difficulties. It is interesting that despite this great success and the extent to which they are enjoying counter cyclical profit, they were still seeking to improve their management activities.

I had worked with this manager and other members of the management team for some time and it was a delight to see that he was still working very much on reinforcing the requirements of **planning** to ensure maximum success in business implementation. The point that he made was in relation to planning being very difficult and an activity often avoided by managers after they have acquired skills in other basic areas, such as initiating work activities, inspiring individuals to perform and installing suitable control systems.

One of the major benefits of having a systematic approach to management overall is being able to then return with extra time available to reconsider the planning process and fine-tune areas of day to day management by improving the systems that are already installed.

As this manager so correctly identified, there is a tendency for managers to feel the job is complete once they have systematically installed all aspects of a complete management system for the first time. In fact, this is only the beginning of the process. It is the fine tuning which is an ongoing activity for the remainder of the manager's working life that characterizes managers who will be very successful compared to those who will do an average job.

Planning is certainly one area where there is a tendency to avoid putting in the time required because of the perception that it is not the stuff that real management is made of. Of course the reverse is true and high quality planning balanced by dedicated implementation are two activities that characterize very successful individuals and organizations.

So, be a thinking manager in your goal achievement process and realize that planning falls into the ounce of prevention being worth a pound of cure category and is a very sound investment. You may even be able to take on the role of the well respected senior manager I have spoken about and remind others of this principle.

I can't find it

How often do you hear people say, 'I can't find it'. That important document that arrived only last week that had been put away for safe keeping has disappeared.

I have always felt very strongly that people do not realize the major negative impact that unsound records management can have on any business. I was fortunate, early in my career, to be introduced to a system where thousands of customer record cards had to be accessed on a daily basis and the words: 'I can't find it' meant that the entire customer record card would have to be rewritten the same day while the customer waited and at great embarrassment to the employee and the organization.

Later, I was involved with an organization that held hundreds of thousands of customer records and had one of the most advanced computerized filing systems available. In addition to appreciating the essential nature of sound records management this also gave me the opportunity to look at the key characteristics of a successful filing system.

The first stage in the development of any filing system is design. Regrettably, many people not only do a poor design but some fail to design it at all, just allowing the filing system to grow up out of nowhere. Designing a filing system requires knowledge of when, why and how the information to be stored has to be accessed in the future.

For this reason, the best person to design the filing system is very often someone who knows a lot about the business but is still able to look at retrieval from a totally fresh point of view. As with all aspects of records management the person doing the designing must be meticulous.

The second stage in records management is documentation. A sound design without thorough documentation is virtually useless. Documentation of how systems work is still one of the areas where so much of business falls down and fails to perform. The computer industry comes to mind immediately in this regard. There can be no better advice in the documentation phase than to keep it simple.

The golden rule of filing is this next stage - do it now. Out of date filing is like a snow ball that accumulates more errors, more frustration and more delay with each out of date document.

The final component of maintaining effective records is to ensure that you review them regularly so that only information which is current and reusable is retained. Naturally, this is part of the original design challenge, but it remains sufficiently problematical for most people that it merits special mention.

The same hard-nosed decision making is required in ruthlessly disposing of materials where the cost of storage is just not warranted for the unlikely event that you will access materials. Naturally, all businesses must maintain their records as required by statute as a first priority. So, design, document, do it now and review and do not be one of those businesses where one of the most common statements is: 'I can't find it'.

Know your costs

One of the oldest sayings in business is, 'The money comes in, and the money goes out'. One of simplest rules in business is that keeping the relationship between the incoming and outgoing in your favor is all that is necessary to have a successful business.

I never cease to be surprised by the number of seemingly successful businesses that are really unaware of what their costs are, particularly in relation to their revenue and their profit.

Many businesses are in the situation where they would be better off just having their investment in a fixed deposit, but their variable (and fixed) costs are so out of control and poorly analyzed that they are not aware of their true (very poor) return on investment.

All businesses from the smallest to the largest should be aware of the true state of their finances. Regrettably, it is now common to find businesses that are going into receivership which have atrocious financial records and would never have been able to anticipate their impending failure purely because of lack of information. So why do these situations occur?

Many business managers justify poor financial management on the basis that they can 'feel' when things are going well or going badly and can take action accordingly. Certainly, a close involvement with the business and knowledge of the market to prompt investigation of problem areas is critical. This management by 'gut feel", however, should be an adjunct and not a substitute for sound financial records and budgeting procedures.

Nothing of what I am saying is particularly new. The business clue is that many people are still backing their own judgment against sound financial sense. If they were the only ones to lose (or if they never lost at all), there might be reason to be less concerned. The critical thing is that these people are often managers from whose decisions some monumental disasters have occurred, leaving hundreds of thousands of people in various states of financial loss. Of course these investors should have been able to expect some greater level of professionalism in relation to their investments, but we will leave that till another day.

The real message that we are looking at here is, that the manager has a responsibility to know about all costs in detail and make well informed decisions about profitability or its absence. It is also worth noting that the advent of complex computer solutions for financial management has not changed this situation. Indeed the complexity of these systems can make the situation worse if the manager has an aversion to computers as well as accounting. Regardless of the systems used, there is never an excuse for ignorance when it comes to the figures. It only requires hard work and attention to detail. There is no magic here, just a lot of hard work.

Don't whinge, change it

In tough times, of which there have been many recently, it is very tempting to just give up the ghost and regard it all as just being too hard. In particular this is the time when many people start looking externally and saying that external factors are to blame for their failures. Certainly, external factors are always very important in any business situation or in any individual endeavor. Nevertheless, it is surprising how many of these factors we can control if we are able to apply our efforts in the right areas.

One of the key factors in changing away from this focus on external influences is to realize that we can alter the environment if we attack it in the right way. I use the word attack on purpose because that is the amount of effort required to achieve any result. So how do we go about achieving the changes that we want? I will list some of my suggestions in general terms and allow you to interpret them to suit your own situation.

In the first instance, it is important to pick the areas of greatest influence in relation to your needs and determine whether or not that external influence is accessible to you. If you know what the external influence is and can 'push back' then you have an opportunity to control your situation. This may involve the appropriate government minister or some other politician. It may be one of your major suppliers. It may be someone in your own organization or it may be the representative of some other major body in the community. In any event, you should identify those individuals who can have the most impact on your circumstances and then develop a strategy for change to meet your needs.

Of course, one of the most important aspects of attempts to change the environment is the development of strategies which indicate clearly that these changes are not only in your interest but in the interest of the wider business community.

Influencing others to change their point of view can be difficult if they stand to suffer significantly through giving up their own stance. For this reason it is important to understand that very often their point of view is held only through force of habit and ignorance of alternative strategies that may be in their interests as well as yours. Nevertheless, in any situation your argument has to be very well presented because in the area of philosophies and business ideals logic appears to have become the weakest argument of all.

Realistically, and unfortunately, it is sometimes necessary to abide by rules such as 'the squeaky wheel gets the most oil' and 'bull dust baffles brains' in preparing a comprehensive argument to win on the day. Preparation in the form of knowing your 'enemy', working towards your goal, and gaining full knowledge of the 'enemy's' strengths and weaknesses, is absolutely essential. As stated earlier, you might feel words like 'attack' and 'the enemy' are a little strong in these circumstances. If you are bleeding (metaphorically) to death, however, from inefficient government regulation, poor customer service or any form of biased business practice, you had better start thinking in battle terms or you and your business will go down the drain.

So finally, remember that the best means of defense is attack and it is amazing how positive you become when you are actually doing something rather than just moaning about the state of play. So get out there and do your ground work, formulate a strategy, attack and you will be surprised how much better you feel. Who knows, you may even find that those around you have been waiting for you to take the initiative and are standing ready to get on board and help you. You definitely will not know until you give it a go. Just remember to review you progress, do not expect unrealistic results and take the time to enjoy what you achieve. Most of all, try to make the process as much fun as the rewards you get from success. You will spend more time getting there than at the goal post, so aim to enjoy the whole experience.

Finding and keeping good employees - part 1

Without a doubt, the finding and keeping of good employees is the secret to developing a good business of any size. Many people are frustrated in their efforts to manage and grow their businesses because they are not able to find employees who will help them to succeed.

Here are some basic initial clues to finding and keeping good employees as part of corporate goal achievement.

Don't Be Scared of Selling Yourself and Your Business Honestly

One of the most basic mistakes people in small business make is underrating the value of themselves and their business as a place to work. Many people are looking for a personal and close knit organization where they can be recognized for the contribution they make and where they don't have to deal with a lot of faceless people. It is important for any small business manager or proprietor to speak positively about the strong points of their business. However, it is also essential to be honest in talking about your business and its future. Don't make promises that you know you won't be able to keep.

Know Your Marketplace

Just as it is your business to know about your products and your competitors, it is very important that you are aware of the employment marketplace for your particular industry. You should acquaint yourself with the quality of performance amongst your competitor's staff and set about recruiting personnel who will give you an advantage in the marketplace. It is also important to know what your business can offer employees in non-financial terms, as this will give you an advantage in recruiting.

If you can identify what makes you special in the marketplace, you will be able to attract better employees and provide a better service, thereby improving your market share and profitability.

Don't Overlook Your Current People

It is less likely in small business that the manager or owner will overlook people currently in the organization for promotion opportunities, but it still happens. The value of your current employees cannot be overemphasized as even in the smaller business, the employees that have been working well in one area may be overlooked for other opportunities as much as they are in large organizations where they are not constantly under the eye of the decision maker.

It is important to realize that employees who already know your business, are committed to you and in whom you have made an investment are the best option for filling more responsible positions. This only applies, of course, if they have the ability and the willingness to make the change. Implementation of a good career path planning system is not limited to organizations with in excess of 500 employees. It is a vital development activity for organizations of all sizes.

The key is to find the time to ask your current employees what they want out of the work situation, whether they would like to advance and what action they would like you to take to help them. Do not be surprised if your team members act surprised when you ask these questions. Despite all the publicity given to benefits of innovative people focused management styles, most employees do not anticipate a high level of care from their boss. This is because the divide between management and workers is a construct that goes back many hundreds of years and is not easily crossed. You will need to be genuine and persistent.

Finding and keeping good employees - part 2

Three further ideas to help you develop your business to its full potential, by helping you find and keep good employees are included here because most goal achievement is about teams.

Recruiting

Filling a properly specified job vacancy requires planning. Careful analysis of job requirements and a specification of the characteristics most needed for doing the job well, can save countless wasted hours 'clarifying' your thoughts while interviewing potential candidates.

Advertising to see who comes forward while 'testing the marketplace' wastes not only the time of numerous confused but genuine job candidates, but also your own time. The task of describing the job, specifying relevant characteristics of the person needed to fill that job, surveying your current employees, and advertising to attract a suitable candidate (if no current employees can fill the job), should be a routine general management activity, but it needs the emphasis and skill of any other management activity.

Using consultants to save your own time or give specialist advice

It is appropriate to engage a consultant to conduct the entire recruitment exercise if the fee is outweighed by the cost of losing time better spent on other activities during the conduct of the recruitment exercise. In many small business situations, the fee may not be justifiable for a total recruitment service. Nevertheless, it may be appropriate to obtain specialist advice on an hourly basis for final interviews and/or psychological testing if a match of the job description and the various candidates' qualifications and experience is not absolutely clear.

Recruit a good backup for success

I have found that organizations which have become very successful after starting as a small business invariably have a high quality person as a 'backup' to the owner or general manager. At a point when the business is looking to grow significantly, it is important to make the decision about selecting a person who has significant experience of the type of growth that the business is likely to experience. Many 'pretenders' will present themselves to see you through this experience. They will be characterized by no previous experience of a similar growth phase and should be avoided at all costs. This is the most difficult time for a business in transition and it takes guts on the part of the proprietor to take on someone who they will normally be in awe of but a good decision here will be one of the most vital made during the life of the business.

Conclusion

Many small businesses stunt their opportunities for growth by not carefully analyzing the return they can get from investing in quality people. Others fear the appointment of quality people because they believe their business would not be sufficiently challenging or interesting. They are waiting for their business to 'grow up'. Businesses will only grow with the addition of better people. Do not be scared to add people who seem too well qualified if it is clear that their experience is appropriate for your future plans. On the other hand, you need to be careful of paying in excess of the candidate's capabilities and beyond your own capacities.

People who are looking to be paid much more than they are worth are famous for using the term 'you pay peanuts, you get monkeys'. You should use the term 'you get what you pay for' and make sure you do exactly that. Small and big businesses alike have failed because of managers or proprietors who are too scared to get close to a new employee very early in the piece to discover if they really are producing results.

The key to successful recruiting is not to sit around for weeks and months waiting for your new employee to produce results, but to detect very early after initial employment whether they are performers or not. If you haven't detected an outcome one way or the other, it means that you are not looking closely enough. In addition remember to recruit people for what you want your business to become not what it is now.

Industrial salvation or deception?

Some time ago I attended an award restructuring meeting at a large factory. The meeting was attended by management, union officials and workers. The aim of the meeting was for union and management to give progress presentations. In particular, they were to present further educational materials in relation to changes in the structure that had already taken place and had contributed to the efficiency of the organization.

Everything seemed to go very well with cooperation between the union and management and the work group sitting quietly (perhaps too quietly) and listening (one assumed) to what was being said. At the conclusion of the various presentations, an open forum to allow free flowing discussion was conducted. Everything went along very smoothly until a man in his 20's wearing blue overalls stood up and let fly.

In this book, I can't repeat the words he used, however the gist of his argument was that he was able to speak freely because he had already resigned and wouldn't be around in a week or two anyway. In no uncertain terms he made it clear that until management got rid of a certain foreman who didn't listen to a word anybody said and was about as resistant to new ideas as a porcupine was to having its spikes brushed backwards with a wire brush, the company was not going to get anywhere.

Furthermore, he gave his opinion that the whole business of award restructuring was a lot of nonsense because efficiency was not going to be affected and the same old work practices were just going to continue and the workers and the company were going to be no better off.

What a breath of fresh air! Talk about letting people know they were rearranging the deck chairs on the Titanic!

Listening to this young man I thought that the only hope one can have is that there are more people out there with the guts to stand up and say what they think. For this to happen, when these organization development activities are going on, is that management and unions have the sense to recognize that these are the people who really care and want Australian industry to succeed. Too often in the past, people like this have been regarded as trouble makers on both sides.

We all have a tendency to resist change, and to go with the flow, but this has to change. We don't all have to experience real pain, but certainly we need to feel some discomfort to know that we are reforming our work processes to achieve a better system and a better end result. Most of the discomfort is associated with the experience of putting effort and plain hard work into the process of improvement.

So the business tip is - don't just play the game and go through the motions. Be prepared to do something and make the reconstruction a real one and you will get the benefits of input from people who see some value in what they are doing.

Review of Planning Principles

- Set realistic goals clearly and confidently.
- Plan your activities and be prepared.
- Stick to the plan.
- Review your progress against the plan.

Add your own. I am sure you will have some.

_____

_____

_____

_____

_____

_____

_____

_____

_____

_____

_____

_____

_____

_____

_____

_____

<u>*Brainstorm on Planning*</u>
<u>*(Have fun with it)*</u>

Chapter Six

Initiate

In this chapter we will consider a range of examples of how taking the initiative is a key part of achieving your goals, both at work and in life generally. The examples will look at the how, why, when and where of being a self starter.

Concentrate and focus

Some time ago I had the pleasure to conduct a number of sessions for a group of young sportspeople.

It was interesting to see how much personal success strategies training did apply to the circumstances of these young people looking to make a career in their chosen sport. Similarly, it seems their various characteristics of commitment; concentration and mental focus certainly have a lot to contribute to success in life.

In talking about concentration and focus, I highlighted several areas for special attention in the personal focus area.

1) Setting goals and working towards their achievement.

2) An <u>obsession about</u> their particular <u>goals</u>

3) A sense of urgency <u>has very often been associated</u> with success and I see it as essential as it contributes significantly to concentration and focus in the achievement of short-term goals.

4) Accepting responsibility for your own actions plus an overall sense of social responsibility.

5) Total concentration and focus.

Anyone can use techniques for personal concentration and focus to achieve goals. As I indicated to this group, it is important to realize that, as with any other skills, these skills must be practiced before there can by any expectation of a positive benefit.

Being a self starter

Most people talk about a person being a self starter, a self motivated individual or having nous as though the person was born with some magical power. Certainly, I am quite often asked by managers to find people with these characteristics when selecting new executives for organizations. Is being a self starter something magical that happens when you are born? I don't think so. Like so many other things associated with being successful, being a performer in the work situation means having the tools necessary to do the job.

Some years ago I decided to expand the standard Position Description used in so many organizations to go beyond the basic list of 'things to do'. I expanded it into a range of areas that included not just <u>what</u> to do but <u>how</u> to do it. Using the headings Plan, Initiate, Innovate, Check and Standardize it was possible for the organization or the individual to include all those 'self starting' characteristics into what I called the Position Responsibility Statement (PRS).

By clearly defining your personal responsibilities for planning your work, initiating your work activity, being innovative in the way you do your job, checking your own work and developing standardized systems of operation for greater efficiency, it is very easy to become a member of that group of self starters. If you sit around waiting for that magic moment to occur when you become a self starter, you will be waiting for a long time. A clearly written PRS, however, lets you set your own guidelines and standards for performance and create the environment where you can make yourself into a self starter. Fill out the PRS at the end of the book to suit any situation.

Organise it and make it happen

It seems to me that the bulk of the problems experienced by the business people I deal with can be grouped into two areas. First, many problems resulted from people having an inability to analyze the situation confronting them and organize themselves and others to cope with it. I recall many years ago hearing about an incident where an acquaintance stepped through a plate glass door and a fixed glass panel behind it. Both panels shattered, showering him in glass and causing horrific injuries. His friends and acquaintances at the function stared in disbelief at their host, a very powerful man, still standing there moments after the glass panels had collapsed. Everyone was paralyzed by disbelief. The host, who would have bled to death without urgent medical treatment, well and truly whipped them into action when he shouted, 'Get organized you bastards!'.

I feel in many ways that the above story is an interesting parallel to the situation that Australia has found itself in so many times since the early 90's. In the 80's, we were quite fit and healthy. That situation changed to not being unlike having stepped through a couple of plate glass panels. More importantly, I think the advice about getting organized is very appropriate to the circumstances of the early 90's and beyond.

Second, I have found that people in business do seem to lack the will to make things happen. So often I have been confronted by senior managers who are frustrated by members of their team who just do not seem able to 'get on with it'. This procrastination or failure to have a sense of urgency has caused a lot of poor performance in many areas of business. It is clearly more than a coincidence that thousands of desk pads throughout Australia have the words 'do it now' emblazoned across them. What we have to do is get the words off the paper and put them into action.

So for Australian business the motto must be: 'Organize it and make it happen', if we are to regain some of the success that has eluded us in the latter part of the last century and early part of this one.

Reminder of Initiate Principles

- **Begin at the beginning.**
- **Organise yourself.**
- **Allocate and apply selected resources.**
- **Look for immediate rewards.**

And room for your own ideas.

_____

_____

_____

_____

_____

_____

_____

_____

_____

_____

_____

_____

_____

_____

_____

_____

_____

Chapter Seven

Innovate

Innovation and the individual

A senior manager I had the pleasure to assess was one of the most intelligent people in all the areas of the assessment that I had ever met. He was also particularly creative. This assessment was part of extensive work conducted for a particular company and I subsequently worked with this senior manager extensively.

One evening we were discussing the company's history of growth and this person tried to summarize, to the best of his ability, the reasons for the founder's outstanding success. He was able to detail the various organizational, economic and experience factors without great difficulty, but still seemed dissatisfied. He then went on to describe his boss's tremendous courage and competitiveness in business but was still not happy that he had the complete answer. T hen he said,

'Sometimes when all the evidence says no, he says yes and most times he turns out to be right. I still think he has a crystal ball under the table that he consults before he decides what to do ' .

So what does this mean for the practical manager who wants to be an outstanding business decision maker? Simply that you have to use all the evidence available in a systematic way but fairly often there will be a need to look inside yourself and just find out what your 'gut feel' is in relation to the problem.

You should not use this as an excuse to escape the hard work of analysis. I can tell you from experience that the outstanding achiever that I have just mentioned was a constant gatherer and analyzer of business information at all levels and I think his crystal ball had a lot more carefully designed electronic circuitry than people generally thought and did not involve as much guess work or magic as might have been imagined. The practical manager prepares thoroughly but is not scared to introduce personal values.

Innovation - it is for everyone

I was asked recently by the manager of a very large organization what more he could do to improve his company's performance. His company was already engaged in a variety of team development activities work with various employees and he felt that his management team was very positive and receptive to new ideas. This company was already involved in all the formal activities of multi-skilling, multi-tasking and industrial reform that was supposed to rejuvenate productivity.

After a lengthy discussion involving mostly a review of activities undertaken previously by the company, the manager decided to put me on the spot with the question: 'Well, what's the answer?'. This manager seemed somewhat taken aback when I advised him to get a full and genuine contribution from his employees. This technique for improved productivity is the same now as it was 20 years ago and is just as well known.

At first he seemed a little skeptical because he thought that the company was already doing this with the various employee groups that they were using. I told him that those employee groups were probably just another substitute for middle management which was no better able to obtain and use information from employees now than it was 20 years ago.

Quite frankly, it comes dressed up and in many guises, but genuine success in large 'value adding' organizations, always involves a healthy dose of employee accountability and contribution through improved communication.

The problem for most organizations, is that their perception is that this is all too simple, that they are already doing this and not getting results. The reality is that they <u>think</u> they are getting to the employees who work in the various areas on a day-to-day basis, but the reality is that they are not.

Being personally resourceful and innovative

It is a fallacy that being innovative or personally resourceful is the province of a very small percentage of the population. All of us have the capacity to be inventive in so many ways. Once we get it clear in our minds that we can think of better ways of doing things we certainly open up a whole realm of new experiences.

It really is as simple as believing that you can and will think of better ways of doing things. One of the major drawbacks of most educational systems is that they educate people not only in the information provided, but to think that everything that is to be thought of has been thought of and being inventive isn't part of the equation.

If you've now reached your 30th, 40th, 50th year or your 90th year for that matter and haven't got that innovative philosophy, don't despair, it really is just a matter of changing your whole way of thinking but starting slowly – strangely enough.

Depending upon your personality, you may want to work independently, by changing some basic home routines. Alternatively, you may decide to study up using any of the numerous books published by authors in the areas of creativity and innovation.

Whatever technique you use, it will almost certainly bring instant results. The real skill is in persisting with your efforts and turning those initial-inspiring experiences into longer-term changes in your style to make you practically resourceful and innovative in the long term.

Develop your own ideas

It was a real pleasure on a factory visit the other day, to hear the manager say that all of the machinery was built 'in-house'.

One of the aspects of Australian industry that is most ignored is the fact that we do so much creative work in many areas. This was just another example of an organization that had decided that rather than buy expensive machinery from overseas they could build it themselves.

In addition to building their own machines, they had made a variety of improvements which made the machinery more efficient and more effective. Another aspect of this particular in-house development activity was the fact that the company had been established in Australia in the last century.

Because I spend so much time introducing new management systems into organizations where middle and senior management has 'atrophied', I was delighted to see an old company that had maintained its innovation and freshness.

Far too often people in companies develop the ROYL syndrome. ROYL stands for Rest On Your Laurels. It is a symptom that arises when people get the feeling that they have done as much as they need to do and can cruise along on the glory of past performances. This is bad enough in itself, but these people often work on the basis that because it took them 20 years to get there, anyone following on behind them should take a similar amount of time. Regrettably, this is one of the major contributors to the creation of large 'dead-spots' in Australian companies, particularly the very large ones.

It is very important for organizations, through their managers, to have the courage to identify individuals who are no longer innovative and unwilling to encourage others in the organization to be innovative. It has long been said that a company is either expanding or retracting and that there is no in-between. If organizations are to continue in an expanding and healthy growth mode, they must identify the dead wood and either bring about a change for new growth or cut it out. Sounds awful I know, but it is a last resort.

This is an area where managers and organizations have great difficulty. I have always approached it on the basis that the pruning of dead wood is the same as pruning a plant, it is done for the benefit of the entire organization. To allow a part of the organization to inhibit the growth of the rest of the organization is an unhealthy business practice. The job of the manager is to provide opportunities for growth at all levels within the organization. A difficult but necessary part of this process is the modification or removal of parts of the organization that are stifling growth.

An unpleasant thing to do, but it does not have to be (and should not be) done unpleasantly. If people no longer match the role required they should be provided with their entitlements and treated with respect and, preferably, a suitable career transition service.

Looking from the other side

I had the most valuable opportunity the other day to do some laboring work in a landscaping gang to help out a friend. In doing organization development exercises, I repeatedly talk about the value of doing interviews with all the staff to get their personal perspective. In this regard, I am often asked, 'Do you think they can really tell us anything about how to run the company?'. Numerous organization development exercises have convinced me that they can, but my experience as a landscape gardener made the same point in a much more convincing way.

Because of poor planning, mostly due to where the various materials had been placed, double and triple handling was the order of the day. Worse still, as the day progressed, the planning did not improve and the output of the labor was about one half to one third as effective as it could be.

I was tempted to make some constructive suggestions about how to improve the overall conduct of the exercise, but realized that because of the mood that had developed in the 'management area', this would not be a wise decision. So I labored on, savoring the 'frustrated employee' syndrome and associated learning experience to the full. The lesson to learn from this whole scenario is that employees do have a lot to contribute, but there can be many barriers to them candidly giving advice on how to do a job better. The removal of these barriers to making good suggestions is one of the all time mysteries for many managers.

To say it is achieved simply by establishing an atmosphere of openness and genuine rapport is to point to one of the biggest challenges in organization development. This is because the idea may be simple, but its execution is anything but.

In installing organization development programs, I have one main theme. Any individual can make any comment and suggestion about any activity the organization undertakes provided that that suggestion is directed towards improving the performance of the overall organization. There are many potential pitfalls in pursuing this ideal, not the least of which is people misinterpreting what constitutes something positive for the organization as a major threat to their power base. Nevertheless, if people can be kept on the right track, the positive atmosphere created by this common goal can achieve significant results.

Engineering excellence gives the edge

The search for the secret of success goes on in so many areas. People are constantly asking 'How do we create a successful product?' 'How do we get into the export market' 'How do we make money?' and so on.

A clear example of success in developing a skill, exporting that skill and having a successful organization was presented to me very recently.

The example featured one of Australia's leading engineering firms. I was speaking to one of their senior directors who had just come back from a long assignment overseas. He was explaining that their level of corporate skill and quality was at such a point that the normally arduous tendering process seemed to be becoming superfluous.

As an example, he explained how the company had received a casual letter from an overseas company enquiring about their expertise in a particular area. They sent back a capabilities statement and a price. Next thing, they received a brief letter telling them what work was required and asking them to make arrangements to do the job.

If only business was that easy for everybody. The reality of course is that this situation featured a lot of really hard work. This engineering consortium has been active in the Australian market place for more than 50 years. They employ some of the most skilled graduates in the country and they have completed some of the most significant work in Australia.

Nevertheless, there have been times when they may well have fallen into a number of traps. Avoiding these pitfalls is what characterizes a successful enterprise. It is clear, that they did not allow their areas of expertise to be determined only by their past experiences. They went to the marketplace and determined what the demand would be in certain areas in the future and developed skills accordingly. They diversified from one particular industry area into other industry areas to offset the impact of a downturn in one of the market's segments in which they were active. Before it became fashionable, they multi-skilled their professionals to allow a much more versatile staffing of major projects. Also, they converted to the use of contract labor to better manage the supply/demand equation long before others.

All of the above strategies amount to good management of an enterprise and good management of the skill base upon which the enterprise relies. The bottom line is of course, that having a great product is no use to you if no-one wants it. As one of my long term colleagues says it's no good selling red tins, when everyone wants blue tins. All of these innovative achievements by this firm are just about 'staying ahead of the game'.

To do it personally you have to concentrate and focus on what makes the difference in the area where you want to excel. Strangely enough, some of the techniques for keeping you mind sharp have been around for a very long time and are epitomized by board games such as chess and mahjong. Once you are on the right track then it becomes all about being persistent in finding new ways of doing things.

Psychology still a luxury

In reading a document recently about the interests and profiles of public company directors, it was disappointing to see reinforced the general philosophy that accounting, law and operations were the prime areas of experience for directors and the main areas of interest pursued by directors. It should not surprise you then that, in a counseling session with a student who had deferred law studies for 12 months with thoughts of pursuing a career in psychology, I was able to confidently say that the psychology/human resources area within business enterprise remains a luxury.

Interestingly, no-one up to the time of our discussion had been able to indicate clearly to this law student why study of the law and a law degree was a good thing from a business point of view. Anyone spoken to had merely shrugged their shoulders and said 'Well, you know, it's a good thing'. A basic examination of the establishment, conduct and winding up of any activity in life gives a clear clue as to the reasons why law is a good thing from a career point of view. Perhaps it is more of a good thing than it should be because of our inability to get past the basics of treating people fairly and with respect.

If you examine the commitment and enthusiasm amongst senior people for the people side of their enterprise, it is often fairly shallow. For many years professionals and company executives in the areas of human resources and related fields have spoken about preaching to the converted and doing business with themselves. Once again, in speaking to a senior human resource professional from one of Australia's largest companies, it was clear that he was not happy with the company strategy of cutting back heavily on human resource activities in all areas. He felt that, at a time when hundreds of people were being retrenched and numerous jobs were being relocated to others states, human resource expertise was needed more than ever.

In government circles as well, the focus is supposed to be on human skill development and empowerment as the way of the future, but development of bureaucratic systems is more and more oriented towards distrust. A multiplicity of systems to reduce individual decision making and responsibility seems to be preferred to development of overall management skills which are measured on effectiveness. The business that perfects the psychology of the enterprise and relates it to overall effectiveness will easily outstrip its competitors. Regrettably, achieving this goal is much more difficult than it sounds and many organizations give up long before they get anywhere near understanding the goal, let alone achieving it.

Computers - deliverance or disaster?

Many years ago I recall introducing high powered computer systems into a large organization where I was employed in a training capacity. I did this with my usual warning that it would increase an individual's capacity to make mistakes as much as process correction transactions. I still believe that being aware of a computer's ability to multiply your mistake making power is the safest way to approach computerization.

One of the largest computer companies in the world has a policy of zero product defects in briefing subcontractors to supply them with components. If users of their products and other computer systems had the same attitude to installation of computer systems, there would be far fewer problems and a lot more profitability.

At the heart of our problem with computers is an interesting phenomenon in our society that I call the 'medical model syndrome'. This phrase is what I use to describe the feeling in our society that all problems should be able to be solved in the same way that a doctor fixes our medical problems using pills. We shouldn't have to do any thinking or take an active role, we merely have to pop the pill and the problem goes away.

Unfortunately, most problems and the solutions that go with them are not like that. Computing is definitely an interactive worker driven solution, but many people still have the medical model syndrome. Also, this situation is often made worse by the presence of computer doctors (or witch doctors!) who would like you to think that the medical model in computing actually works.

I recall one large organization that purchased a very expensive system which was to be the solution to all their computing problems. It was a turnkey situation, that is, you turn the key, and drive the system immediately. Unfortunately, the system was still sitting 'by the edge of the road' a full year after the key was turned. It had turned out to be more of a TURKEY situation than a turnkey one. This sort of situation illustrates beautifully why my one major recommendation to anyone buying a computer system (whether it is micro or mammoth) is to ask one very important question of the potential supplier. That question is: 'Where can I see this system currently being used successfully for exactly the type of operation that I intend to use it for?'. A study of your intended system in use elsewhere is like test driving a car. You can check all the features, see how it performs and ask a current owner for an assessment of performance. This sounds simple, yet it amazes me how many people will purchase an extremely expensive computer system without even asking for this type of information. In fact, some people feel that a comment such as 'You will have the first system installed of this type, making you a pioneer!' is actually positive. Imagine if someone said that they were going to sell you a car that had never been out on the road, had not been road tested, did not have complete instructions, did not have a workshop manual and had no spare parts. You would probably fall over laughing; yet people buy computer systems in these circumstances and wonder why they will not work. So, if you are buying a computer system, look for reliability, look for a track record and make sure you have personnel who are competent to supervise and maintain that computer system and are able to give you all the professional services in design, documentation and implementation that are necessary.

Australia's Unrecognised Talent

I was addressing a group of managers the other day who are currently undergoing the delights of Total Quality Management. Having spoken to them for an hour on 'Issues In Management' and not having mentioned Total Quality Management once, they may have been suspicious that I didn't know what it was. My rather quick answer to the question of what TQM amounted to was that it was a product that was created in Australia in the 1920's and re-imported in the 1980's at great expense to management.

This was of course a fairly glib and somewhat simplified retort in relation to the development of the total concept of Total Quality Management. Nevertheless, there is a very serious element in this view about Total Quality Management or, as it is now more often called, Quality Management. Australia will probably go down in history as the country that wasted more good ideas and people than any other country in the world. Despite having well recognized leaders and techniques in areas such as medicine, engineering, communications, literature and film, Australia continues to pour billions of the country's hard earned dollars down the drain of externally produced resources, with an enthusiasm that defies the imagination.

Although it may seem like it, I am not putting forward an elaborate argument for buying Australian made and tariffs. I believe people should be free to buy whatever they choose from wherever they choose. What I am putting forward is an argument for producing competitive Australian made by the investment of Australian capital in worthwhile ideas. People involved in this area will immediately say, 'Doesn't this idiot know anything? All the states and territories have numerous programs to help manufacturers with good ideas become viable'. Yes, there are numerous people employed to help and stimulate Australian industry, but let us consider the form of this help.

Australia is very successful in cricket, rugby league, rugby union and various other sports. What experience do the coaches and administrators in these sports normally have? Very rarely will you find that they are professional public servants designed to help these sports people succeed. They are usually previous representative champions. They have been there and they have done it.

I believe Australia's success in these various sporting fields is in no small way associated with the fact that the people who develop new up and coming talent are themselves talented, are able to recognize talent and have the ability to nurture and refine that talent to world class standards. All of this brings us back to Total Quality Management. If you wish to identify quality, develop it and bring it to world class standards, I argue that you have to have been there and done it yourself. Quite frankly, the people associated with the assessment and development of new talent in business in Australia haven't even been there, let alone done anything. It is small wonder that so much Australian talent goes unrecognized.

Business bureaucracy - double aaagh!

On another occasion, I wrote about the type of bureaucracy that we all experience at some time or another in attempting to deal with large government organizations. In doing so, I used a single example just to illustrate how dramatically 'thickheaded' some of these organizations can be and bring anyone's blood to the boil.

Having already become excited about the subject, I was much more concerned when I was told the other day by a business leader, that his decisions about expansion and general business development were increasingly being negatively influenced by the growth in government bureaucracy in his industry.

It is important for me to make the point that this individual has for a long time been a leader in his field. As such he has put pressure on government to introduce meaningful changes that have developed his industry, improved safety and provided a better service for the general public. For this reason, I was all that more surprised by his vehement attack on burgeoning bureaucratic processes.

What was really frightening about this conversation was this executive's comment that he feared taking any action or making any statement in relation to this increase in bureaucratic involvement because of possible reprisal against which he would have no recourse. I am used to hearing these types of comments from people who are relatively powerless in dealing with large bureaucracies and I am well able to understand the realism of their fears having worked in a variety of roles on both sides of the fence. When a senior business leader makes these types of comments in relation to Government, however, it is time to start worrying.

Government without integrity is tyranny, no matter how politely and numbingly that tyranny may be applied. In business, it is essential to remain involved in Government processes. Usually, this is by means of appropriate industry organizations, professional groups and unions, depending upon the individual's role.

The important aspect of this involvement through an organization or individually is to maintain the perspective of analyzing processes on the basis of their efficiency and effectiveness. That is, how well are they conducted and what contribution do they make to the end result? If bureaucratic processes are inefficient or irrelevant to the development of the community, they need to be analyzed, redesigned and modified. Regrettably, bureaucracy has a penchant for undertaking these processes for their own sake and maintaining control over them, thus ensuring that the 'right' conclusion is reached.

Only appropriate involvement by outside individuals and organizations can combat this natural tendency to take action to ensure the survival of the bureaucracy. So as difficult as it may be, hang in there and fight business bureaucracy where it is losing relevance or is inefficient. Work to facilitate the development of bureaucracy that supports the community by doing relevant and efficient work. The bottom line is: if you don't like it, complain in the grateful knowledge that you live in a community where complaining won't cost you your freedom or your life.

Old ways hard to eradicate

It was staggering to hear recently of a leading corporation that was undergoing its second restructure within two years and moving away from a very flat management structure to rebuild the pyramid that existed two years before.

Change for the sake of change I thought had disappeared, as had newly appointed senior executives imposing their will on organizations purely to show 'who is boss'. It certainly seems this is not the case. One of the most frustrating things for employees is the inability to gain access to senior people because of tangled corporate structures. To see people creating this tangled web as a new strategy for success sends a chill up my spine.

Apparently the feeling and talk in this organization already is that people further <u>down</u> in the organization will sink deeper. Having worked for ten years to eliminate the mushroom syndrome (keep them in the dark and feed them on compost), I can only hope that employees now are more personally able to express their disquiet.

Another option is to join the majority and just ride the wave and not swim against the current. The only trouble is that the wave and the boat riding it, only has seats for ten people and there are hundreds in the water.

A bit dramatic perhaps, but one has to dramatize sometimes to get some awareness of just how downtrodden people can become in a hierarchical or pyramid system of management.

As one of my senior consultants is so fond of saying: 'There are still people who are using management techniques that were invented in the same year as the pop up toaster and they are still out there in positions where they can have the same negative impact they had twenty years ago.' So time brings positive changes for some, but for others, retrograde steps are still being taken that lose track of the bigger picture and ignore the benefits of allowing people to take responsibility and develop at all levels.

Hopefully there will not be too many 'throwback managers' who will lead us back to the age of the dinosaurs. However, employees have to be active in developing their skill levels to combat these problems. Alternatively, with good skills, employees can move to more productive organizations with informed management styles that make good use of the employees' skills.

Rapid expansion

A question that people often ask me about successful businesses that I have consulted to is: 'How did they get to be so big from such a small beginning?'. This is a question I love answering because people are normally stunned by the simplicity of the first few points but totally disillusioned by the mysteriousness of the last.

First, and almost invariably, an individual with a vision and a severe case of single mindedness is involved in every business which grows rapidly and successfully into a large corporation. This single mindedness is normally complemented by a burning desire to prove something to someone. That someone can be a particular individual or group and can be real or symbolic of some policy or idea.

Generally, the successful individual will have an obsession that results in a phenomenally high work output from long hours of work and apparently unrealistic expectations of associates and subordinates. It also results in a higher level of risk taking.

Second, the individual or group that takes a small company to success in the large corporate sector is generally willing and able to locate, recruit and work with the best people and techniques available for their particular industry. This particular characteristic is the embodiment of internalizing the old saying 'You'll never fly with eagles if you work with turkeys'. There is also no fear of paying the right price for the best talent. In fact, being better than the entrepreneur in a skill that is vital to the new business is perceived as a decided asset for all new subordinates, colleagues and consultants.

Finally, there is the mysterious aspect of being successful in expanding a business. Those entrepreneurs and business developers that have been successful seem to have two additional characteristics. Apart from working hard and being dogmatic, they seem to have the ability to fall in the cream and pick a winner. Although the formula remains 99% perspiration and 1% inspiration, the picture is not complete without both commodities and there are plenty of hard working dogmatic people who are still running very small businesses or who have gone broke. So crystal balling and good old fashioned luck still have some hand in the fortunes of those highly successful individuals who build big businesses from humble beginnings.

So how does the average 'battler' acquire these attributes? For points one and two, start relearning from childhood. For point three, go back and be reborn. Sound hard? So is being an outstanding success!

Innovation Techniques

Innovate to identify strategies to maximise effectiveness.

Innovate to succeed.

HOW TO INNOVATE

- **Always look for a better way.**
- **Disassemble and reassemble the task/activity/process.**
- **Relax and visualise.**
- **Focus on the outcome.**

Chapter Eight

Check

A close friend of mine, Brian Griffin, has a favourite saying. 'Measure twice, cut once'. Now he was an apprentice and tradesman before he became a manager and successful business owner, so this is old knowledge. The problem is that it is old and true knowledge that still gets forgotten on a regular basis. If you want to reach your goals, the small things that you check yourself and teach other people to check are going to make the difference.

Efficiency - where did it go?

Many years ago industry had a relatively brief flirtation with activities known as Work Study and Efficiency Analysis. Fairly quickly, they achieved notoriety as being one of the classic symbols of big brother looking over your shoulder. Through a variety of scenarios, this activity in its most basic form faded into the sunset, but I fear that we may have thrown the baby out with the bath water.

Many years ago I had the unenviable job as a new graduate of doing an efficiency analysis on a particular department of a large public sector organization. This department provided a support service to thousands of other people in the organization. It had transformed suddenly from a highly efficient reliable department into a total disaster which was incurring the wrath of the staff and management of every other department in the organization. Upon investigating the circumstances of the decline in efficiency in this service department, I realized that I had to adopt a 'time and motion study' approach. There was no one doing any checking of the process who could advise me of the performance standards.

In addition, no one was going to assist me amongst the 25 staff in finding out what the problem was. It was a most uncomfortable environment. Interestingly, I discovered the problem very quickly merely by scanning the number of active files that were held awaiting action. Because of the layout of the work area, it was very easy to see that one particular individual was the bottleneck in the whole operation.

As it transpired, this particular individual had been recently appointed without an appropriate selection process and was not at all competent to perform the duties of the position. It would have been particularly easy if the difference between this individual's work performance and the work performance of the rest of the group was all that needed to be reported. But this was not the correct approach. It was necessary to determine this individual's performance against pre-determined standards to ensure a fair and equitable resolution. Furthermore, It was not the fault of this individual that the appointment had been made inefficiently.

The most significant aspect of this activity was the unwillingness of the various individuals involved within the department to come to grips with what constituted efficiency and competence. It transpired that the managers in the department, upon being questioned, were very uncomfortable with assessing the work of their subordinates and had never done any analysis of workflow. This was all the more significant because analysis of the workflow was very easy because of the nature of the work. In fact, the analysis took less than 48 hours because of available data and the situation was resolved within five working days.

One of the most concerning aspects of this particular incident so long ago is the presence of similar circumstances in many areas of industry today. It seems that we have made little advance in this area and that we may actually be creating certain protected areas where a quantitative assessment of performance is ruled out for emotional or political reasons with subsequent negative impact on the performance of the organization.

I believe this negative approach to efficiency generally is a result of managers inability to implement activities such as work analysis and performance appraisal in a fair and humane manner. It seems that the old age of 'fair, firm, friendly, but not familiar' remains very relevant to the area of performance analysis, but still eludes many people. Globally, the need is still to have the courage to look at individual workers level of competence, discuss this with them and then take action in conjunction with the individuals involved. This is the only fair and effective way to get the best overall performance for the organization - by matching the challenges to the ability of the individuals involved.

Commitment - where are we at?

Australians have always been fiercely proud of being able to say, 'I'm no bludger'. While I am sure the meaning of this statement has changed somewhat over the years, I think it currently can safely be interpreted as saying: 'I don't let the team down; I do my fair share; I pull my weight and so on.' So just how good is the Australian worker these days?

I am often asked by managers about inconsistency in work performance in their work group. Typically, one or two members of the group do not have the same level of commitment and do not put in the same effort as the rest. When this issue is raised in training sessions, as it often is, responses range from: 'Sack 'em' through to 'You should manage around them'. This problem centers around one of the most difficult things to ever achieve in life generally - equity. Things will never be completely equitable or fair, because fairness is an emotional concept.

Determining what is fair in the work environment is a very personal thing. It is amazing how the work group will overlook very poor performance or low effort on the part of members of the group in some circumstances and will be totally intolerant of it in others.

The reasons for this are invariably emotional. So, in order to achieve balance in the work environment, the manager must work very closely with each team member to arrive at an understanding in relation to what constitutes reasonable effort. Despite my comments that this concept is so heavily emotionally based, I must emphasize most emphatically that developing a basis for discussion of work performance in factual terms is essential to achieving success in management of group performance. The emotional aspects will not disappear, but without a basis of discussion centering on work output and other observable factors, it will not be possible to discuss realistically what is regarded by the manager as unacceptable performance on the part of a member of the team.

A very interesting dilemma in this area, is the changing work environment brought about by changing economic circumstances. When things get tough, many people who have been paid high levels of salary are no longer able to deliver that level of value to the organization. While managers are able to perceive this difficult circumstance, they find it very difficult to convey the logic and philosophy to the individual concerned and very often look for other ways of removing them from the organization. Any action in this area should be based on a careful analysis of the work value supplied by the individual. The reason this is most often avoided is because the manager has no idea of the concept or finds its implementation just too difficult.

So if you are confronted by someone who you think is not giving you value for money, then come to grips with work value and prepare yourself to discuss with them what you require and why you believe that is reasonable in the circumstances. Then prepare yourself to listen to their argument, it may be more convincing than your own. No matter what the outcome, prepare to be involved in one of the most difficult aspects of business management.

Oh no, not 'it's not my job' again!

For many years I have been teaching the basic principle that everyone in an organization should do what they can to contribute to the success of their company. For example, if an accounts clerk is driving to work at a manufacturing organization and this person passes one of the company's delivery trucks and notices that the tarpaulin that is covering the load has come loose and exposing the load to the weather or may result in loss of part of the load, they should take action. This might be by dropping in to dispatch on the way through to their office and advising an appropriate person who can radio the driver to correct the problem. There are many such examples of going the extra step to help one's colleagues and the organization.

A classic case in point is looking lost or ignored in a theme park, restaurant or hotel. In the hospitality industry, I have the view that everyone who enters your premises, however large or small, is your guest no matter what your job. If you are entertaining at home and one of your guests comes to you as you are putting the finishing touches on the meal and enquires after the location of the toilets, I'm sure you don't say, 'Do you mind waiting fifteen minutes until I finish the meal, then I will have stopped being the cook and I can return to my job of being general host.'

Ridiculous! It could not happen' I can hear you saying to me now. Wrong! I was at one of Australia's most celebrated sports venues as a guest in the now famous 'corporate box'. I was sitting on the aisle seat and an attendant came by and said, 'Have you finished with that?', while pointing to my platter of partially consumed food. 'No' I said, 'but I wonder if it might be possible to get a light beer?' Then bingo, I learned that division of labor was alive and well regardless of what the guest needed. I don't handle that' he said', 'you will have to ask one of those girls up there', pointing up into the crowd about 20 rows further back. At least that explains it, I thought.

What did it explain? Well, I thought it unusual when I arrived that the various personnel were still cleaning out the boxes and laying out the various napkins, cups and other utensils. Up until that time I had also thought it quite unusual that there was a lengthy delay in receiving and a long wait between, the various food servings. After the beer incident and the arrival of the last food serving ten minutes before the conclusion of the game, I finally got my mind off the game long enough to notice that it was all part of an overall picture. This was a not very pretty picture of lack of understanding, lack of skill and lack of management competence.

A few readers have commented that they would prefer me to use positive stories to illustrate my points, because they find them more motivating. I try to use a balance of both positive and negative to give a true indication of my personal observations about the 'state of the nation' so to speak. But just to ensure that I don't leave you too depressed, I went to the opening of a new theme park the other day and the standard of service was absolutely excellent, but more about that another day.

For the time being, I would just like to remind you that when you have guests at your organization or venue, they are everyone's guests, not just the guest of those who are assigned a particular role on the day. You should do everything that you can to help them have either a productive or an enjoyable time, depending on their goals.

Old habits die hard

There was some trade work undertaken on our building recently by a representative of a well known public authority. The majority of the work was completed in service areas which are not frequented by the public, but I went down to have a look at what alterations had been made to allow the installation of new equipment. The sight that greeted me in the service area reminded me of one the oldest bugbears of the Australian work system.

Having completed their work, the people involved had left their rubbish where it fell. For some reason or other, early in the history of the Australian contracts service experience, the 'right' to leave a large mess behind you when you finish the job was created. The most worrying aspect of this behavior is not that it is untidy, but that it is unsafe.

In doing accident prevention training over many years, I have always emphasized that untidy and unsafe work practices are also inefficient work practices and can often be an indicator of underlying problems within the organization. On a positive note, recent legislation would appear to finally address this whole scenario and give some hope for improving the overall performance of industry. Regrettably, the government passes the legislation, but its own operatives very often remain the large group least affected. This is because the 'Physician heal thyself' philosophy applies as much, if not more, to government in a whole range of other areas.

So what has all this got to do with business? Briefly, if someone does a job for you and leaves sharp pieces of wire lying around in areas where other people will later be working, think about sending them a bill for cleaning up the mess. They certainly would have sent you a bill if they had to clean up someone else's mess before they could start work. I am not suggesting that you actually send an account, because you will not get anywhere. I am just saying think about it, and think about the implications. It may affect your attitude very positively about certain services that are provided to you and your overall philosophy about efficiency in services you provide and how you run your own business.

The whole process of checking the job means checking that it is finished. It cannot be finished if it is surrounded by a mess. The more important question to ask, finally, is how can a person regard their work as complete until the final clean up is done? The goal should be to leave a perfect end result because of the personal reward this brings.

Oh, the hypocrisy of it

A government purchasing group conducted a public session recently to educate potential suppliers in relation to their requirements. One of their major requirements for products and services was substantial Australian content. The representative of my organization who was in attendance was optimistic, but skeptical, knowing how these words often ring very hollow in execution. Nevertheless, he was attempting to keep an open mind.

Can you believe that upon being given a purchasing information folder for a particular department and lifting the flap to read the contents, the first words that he read under the flap were: 'Made in England'. What can one say? What can one do? When the tunes that large government enterprises sing for their suppliers are not the ones they dance to, credibility is gone. The paper was not even recycled.

We have our own government bleating about how unfair other government corporations are to us as a state or a nation. I wonder if that is where they learn about how to treat their own constituents? On a positive note, I recall a very senior director from a large company making it very clear that locally made applied as much to the people that they hired as to the products that they brought. In his case, he practiced what he preached, but then he did have total control over the business enterprise.

How do we bring some change to this hypocritical situation, which has the double whammy of not only spending the people's money on overseas products, but has the people's representatives telling local voters who want to be suppliers that they must have significant local content to sell to the government?

Unfortunately, the answer is not an easy one. The difficulty of working with governments and supplying to governments is virtually legend. The fact that our system is such that many are allowed to believe that they are the master and we are the servant does little to help the situation. Fortunately, some Chief Executives have very enlightened attitudes and are bringing about significant changes in attitude.

In the final analysis, it must go back to individuals and their representative groups to keep pushing the barrow of the interests of the community. I know that one major supplier is publicly pursuing that strategy at the moment. Each of us, in whatever way is available to us, must make our thoughts known and encourage the consideration of options which are in the best interests of the community. After all we supply the funds and own the enterprise.

Average is just not good enough

People ask me constantly why the country is in such a hopeless state. The answer is really very simple. Right across the country all Australians see themselves as doing their bit. 'I'm doing just as much as the next person' is the standard philosophy of most Australians. This statement is true. The problem is that average is just not good enough.

The reason that average is just not good enough is because the Australian average is well below average when compared to our competitors in other countries. We have graduates who believe that when they finish their three or four years training they are then entitled to a high paying job which requires them to do no more than just an average day's work. We have people who have been employed for many years who believe that this has given them the entitlement to do just an average day's work.

Unfortunately, this philosophy has caught up with us well and truly. The worst part of it is that the last people to be hit by the catch-up are the very people who caused the need for it - the people who believe that they are already doing their bit. Because of the security of their situation, because of the longevity of their employment and because of their education, they will be the last to be badly affected. By the time this happens, however, they, their families and the rest of the country will well and truly have prepared a second rate country to live in and to hand on to the next generation.

So how do we get ourselves out of this hole? The answer is both simple and difficult. The simple part is the development of a new set of behavior patterns orientated towards achievement and success. The difficult component of this is the pain associated with acquiring those skills. An interesting parallel can be drawn with the acquisition of a ideal state of personal physical fitness. Everybody wants to look and feel good, but nobody wants to do the exercise and eat the good food associated with achieving that result.

The development of our work ethic is absolutely identical. Everybody wants to have lots of money and be well off, but nobody wants to do the hard work necessary to achieve their goals. Carrying on the parallel with physical fitness, change is only going to be achieved if much better work group structures, identical to the team work associated with gaining physical fitness, are introduced into the work situation.

Organizations with the correct work ethic that are successful need to be developed and need to take over those areas which have become sluggish and fail to perform. In the end it comes back to the natural leaders in the community and in business to take up this role. We can only hope that their moral fiber and personal determination is equal to the task.

Quality assurance be damned, price is the key

The response to my criticisms of quality management has been most interesting. A senior executive, who recently retired from a very large organization rang, rang to tell me how he had been making similar comments to his organization for years as it progressively suffered from reducing revenue and reducing profit while introducing every conceivable form of external quality system.

In his view, the company and its executives had lost the plot and were not prepared or able to take responsibility for the performance of the organization. They used these external systems, he said, as crutches and they were completely unsuccessful in their attempts to prevent further decline in the performance of the organization. Closer to home, an academic colleague of mine sent me some literature and gave me the example of a local firm that had invested quite some money in taking out externally certified quality assurance. They discovered, however, that it didn't matter who had quality assurance in supplying for the government, because the lowest price still won the tender, without an assurance system.

As another bizarre example, I was told about a fictitious company that had been set up with nothing more than name and a quality assurance certificate. This organization put in spectacularly low bids and also won the business, before revealing that it did not exist. My academic friend is scathing about industries needing to waste spectacular amounts of money on having other people tick the box to indicate that they are able to produce a product at a level that is satisfactory for the consumer. A scam, a racket, a fad or just a large group of well intention people trying to help industry - what is quality management?

One of my clients loved to talk about a bank that was incredibly well intentioned, worked incredibly hard and managed to lose $2.4 billion. The quality management area has a lot of the characteristics of this bank. A lot of process, a lot of good intent, a lot of money changing hands and a lot of feeling very good in a huge fog that normally occurs when hot air meets cold hard cash. The bottom line is that there are numerous companies around whose products are essential to the community but do not have quality assurance. No-one is shutting them down. Similarly, the lowest price is still winning the bid and no-one is asking those companies if they have quality assurance. Companies are still getting into trouble even though they have quality assurance, but nobody is talking about that.

All in all, quality management and many things associated with it still have the characteristics that my senior executive was so pleased to point out. It's all about people not wanting to take responsibility for general management of their organization. They opt out and go for third party endorsement rather than going with the old saying that 'the buck stops here'. In this regard, the buck stops all over the place. It has to because so many companies are just not doing any good no matter what sort of external certification they have.

If you want to succeed in business take personal responsibility for how your company performs. You need to produce a product that people want and will buy from you because it is good. Your reputation will be based on being a good manufacturer, supplier and service organization, not because an agency has given you their seal of approval. In the final analysis, commerce and industry is about a free market. Quality management in all its forms is just another government impost that reduces the bottom line and keeps money away from shareholders and from employees. Fortunately, there seems to be a strong ground swell of senior managers and business proprietors who agree with this proposition and it may well be as my academic friend indicated, 'Merely a fad that will last several more years and then disappear leaving nothing of any value in its wake '.'

Quality is not complicated

Currently there is a lot of intense discussion about the difficulty and expense of obtaining quality certification. Quality managers are being appointed on all sides, consultants abound and there is a flurry of activity where none existed before. Despite all this intense activity and good intent, many companies still fail to achieve the certification which they are seeking. It has been suggested to me that in many cases it is because a mountain has been made out of a molehill. A senior operations manager who has installed quality systems on a variety of sites and has achieved certification first time, every time believes that the KIS Principal (mostly known as the KISS principle) is still the way to go. This particular manager Keeps It Simple (KIS) and consistently hits the jackpot. On one occasion, he tells me, the system was so simple that he was not sure that it even warranted certification. Nevertheless, because it was a documented true representation of the circumstances and met the requirements, he went ahead. Sure enough despite, and perhaps because of, almost painful simplicity certification was forthcoming.

Interestingly, a colleague of this individual in the accounting area was able to put forward similar experiences at general management level. He had worked as a troubleshooter in a variety of companies and found that invariably they had come to grief by straying from the KIS message. Well dressed senior executives with voluminous reports had led these companies to implement strategies which were hugely unsuccessful. In his view, just a basic dose of common sense could have saved the companies, but they pursued relentlessly the 'bells and whistles' strategies that had been supplied to them by their elegantly tailored senior executives. So, after laboring the point to hammer home the KIS message, I hope it is clear that quality assurance certifications or the quality of general management strategies are decided not by the weight of the materials, but by their content.

Basically, if you cannot understand it, you cannot certify or use it. In other words, an understandable, simple and probably cheap system beats a weighty, complicated and probably very expensive system, every time.

Quality must be total

On a recent plane flight, I was very surprised to find that the plastic wrapped cutlery set that I was given with my meal was dirty. In fact, one of the spoons had a 2cm wide rust stain and I was obliged to scrape food residue from the knife before I could use it. Quite apart from any issues associated with health regulation in the catering area, I was appalled that a major Australian company could allow such glaring lapses in quality.

To my further surprise upon arrival, I found that my luggage, that is normally Priority tagged, was not available as usual. It eventuated that the appropriate tagging procedure had not been completed with a resulting delay in my departure from the airport.

Until our largest companies understand that quality must be total and that any deviation from perfect performance spells a total failure of the system, Australia will continue to lag in international competition. So how do we achieve this level of perfection? Well for a start, we have to start taking ourselves seriously and stop paying lip service to management ideologies like 'Right First Time' that have been around for longer than most modern executives have been alive, let alone working in business.

Universally, we are too inclined to use other famous cliches such as 'Everybody Makes Mistakes' and: 'Murphy's Law Applies'. We need to hold ourselves accountable to a higher standard, not because someone says so, but because of the feeling of achievement this brings.

For their part, business leaders need to be aware that perpetuating philosophies that excuse poor performance is not an acceptance of the inevitable, but a decision to tolerate a lesser standard than is achievable, purely because they are not prepared to make the effort. Regrettably, acceptance of lower standards of this type is so deeply ingrained in our society that we even have a universal cultural excuse based on our right to be different. After all, aren't we living in a free country?

Prevention of these sorts of problems runs on two levels. As a society we have to develop a greater appreciation and demand for perfection and as individuals we need to develop a greater commitment to and ability to produce perfection.

To dispel the criticisms relating to the word perfection, I would point out that perfection is only making a product or service appropriate for use. So in other words, don't have rust stains on your spoons and don't have food baked onto your knives if you are going to run a successful airline.

Quality sells

One of the discussions I have most frequently with my customers is in the area of premium pricing or selling quality. We all talk about being prepared to pay more for a better product and many of my customers sell very high quality products or services that are priced higher than their competitors. One great difficulty that arises with premium pricing of products is the inability of the average salesperson to present the product properly and close a contract at the right price.

I recall speaking to the sales representative of one particular customer, who readily admitted to me that numerous people would only deal with his company, even though the product was more expensive, because they wanted the security of buying the best.

Unfortunately, this particular representative was not able to carry that philosophy into the selling situation. When the customer raised objections, the representative responded by suggesting a reduction in price. This representative was uncomfortable with the selling situation because of a lack of skill in the area of selling quality.

When a customer raises an objection such as, 'The price seems particularly high', they are not saying, 'I want the price reduced'. What that customer is saying is 'I want you to tell me why this product is so much better than other products I have seen at cheaper prices.' The sales representative who does not know that quality sells reacts by reducing the price and conveying the message to the potential purchaser that their product is not any better. This confuses the prospect into thinking that the representative must have been lying about the product being better, because the price was reduced, rather than the representative reaffirming the quality.

A well managed company with a sound marketing and sales philosophy will price a product according to its quality. A skilful sales representative will present the quality of that product in the market place and sell the product at the price appropriate to its quality.

So remember, quality sells. If you have a quality product that has been correctly priced by your organization and you cannot sell it, it will more likely be that you lack the necessary sales skills to present that quality, rather than that the potential customer is thinking that the quality is not there. In addition, there are personal lessons to be learned about yourself and how well you understand what quality means to you and your customers. Putting yourself in the customer's shoes is easy. Just go ans buy something of quality that you really want but think is 'too expensive'.

Don't be scared of figures

Many managers have a fear of getting close to their employees because they are not sure or confident about how they will handle a confrontation when an employee's performance is not up to the standard that is prescribed. Similarly, individuals, when setting standards for themselves, avoid clearly defining their targets because of fear of failure.

The goal of the Practical Manager must be to remove this failure avoidance orientation from the initiating and goal setting behavior of the individuals in the work group. To do this, the manager must gather as much information as they can about the previous history of the job to carefully analyze what the likely outcomes are of setting different goals.

I had an extremely interesting experience in this area which emphasized the importance of history in setting goals and developing success-oriented behavior rather than failure avoidant behavior in individuals. A management team that I consulted to was particularly successful on a global basis. One particular sales manager avoided identifying his group's performance in strictly quantifiable terms, however, despite all of my encouragement to do so. Perceiving this as a particularly difficult individual problem for him, I arranged to meet with him on a one on one basis in an attempt to identify the source of the problem.

It turned out that he was a fairly quiet individual who was quite intimidated by the other more aggressive sales managers in the group and was most uncomfortable with boasting about his group's achievements. Unfortunately, this had flowed on to his reporting habits and he did not even let the figures speak for themselves, having developed a total mental block about individual performance assessment.

After ascertaining that the problem indeed existed, I personally analyzed the history of his performance in the company in terms of his individual and group sales figures. The results of this work were most illuminating. It showed quite clearly that this very quiet sales manager was extremely competent. Not only had he consistently exceeded targets set by senior management on a national basis but he and his group had personally expanded the business in their sector at quite a remarkable rate.

What was most fascinating was seeing his reaction when the sales figures and my written analysis were made available. He had absolutely no problem comprehending the significance of the materials. Further, he immediately started to identify other areas where the figures had particularly positive significance, although this was not obvious to me because of my limited experience in his area of specialization.

Producing that first set of figures opened the floodgates to this particular sales manager. He not only went on to use them on a regular basis in his dealings with management and the members of his team for reporting purposes, but used them as a motivational tool to supplement his already very strong leadership skills in both the technical and sales aspects of product promotion and selling.

Global performance indicators

More and more businesses are looking to focus their attention on one particular measure that indicates how successful the business will be if all members of the enterprise can relate their input to this Global Performance Indicator (GPI). In other words, instead of waiting till they have finished their financial year and checking on their results, these business are looking to find an ongoing indicator that will predict that they are on line to achieve or exceed their financial targets.

One of the very good things about this trend has been its application in non profit areas. These public service oriented organizations have been able to measure their performance on an ongoing basis by working to a single measure of customer satisfaction. One of the major challenges in this area is to find a realistic measure, like customer satisfaction, and then face up to the fact that the organization's is well below where it should be.

As an example, the level of violent crime is a sound global indicator of government performance. By and large, government is charged with the responsibility of managing a society that is physically and mentally safe for its customers, the general public. Similarly, in the transport area, both private and public organizations are charged with transporting individuals and goods from point A to point B safely and on time. In fact, the quality, quantity and safety rules are very powerful in terms of creating any performance indicator.

One very well known international firm has based its whole performance assessment system on providing the right product (quality) in full and on time (quantity), and achieved outstanding results. At the other end of the scale, the non-violent crime performance indicator for government is all about safety, but is still very powerful.

The key strategy for business is to examine their product or service and determine a global indicator. On a trial basis, the global performance indicator should be checked against other retrospective measures of performance. When the global performance indicator has been validated to be a true predictor of success, it can be used as an ongoing measure of the organization's or individual's performance related activities. One of the major benefits of having ongoing performance indicators is the immediacy of the reward to individuals within the organization who, more often than not, have felt quite removed from any results the organization achieves.

For this reason, the global performance indicator is often reinforced with numerous other indicators for smaller working groups and finally individual performance indicators, which link back through the system to the global performance indicator. Of course with such outstanding results being achieved by business that have made successful use of this concept, there has been a flood of consultants building related implementation programs. The problem with these programs is their complexity. If you are thinking complex equals expensive then you are right. The core concept is simple. You just need to identify something that is simple to understand, easily measurable that everybody in the organization can help achieve.

Delivering your customer the products they wanted when they wanted them is one example. Everyone from the sales team to the dispatch team can see where they fit in and can make sure they do their bit. Many major gains were made using this system when phone order takers stopped promising the delivery of orders they knew would not arrive on time. Other changes followed and made this business the market leader.

The most important thing of all is to not be put off by jargon and realize that the development of these measures can <u>lead</u> to outstanding performance. So get yourself a global performance indicator and be one of the modern managers who can look ahead with certainty instead of looking back in disbelief.

Direction in leadership

I visited a garage the other day which is well known for its efficiency, high quality work and racing of performance cars. They must also be one of the few service stations remaining in Australia that opt for driveway service. I have also noticed about this particular service station that the staff are always attentive, well informed and sales orientated.

The owner/operator has exactly the same characteristics which I thought must account, to a significant extent, for the characteristics of his staff, but I thought there must be something more to the success of this organization. Recently, I had the opportunity to find out.

As I was paying my account, I had the time to note the working area of the owner/operator, which is just adjacent to the service counter. Its efficiency in terms of layout, location and general tidiness was most impressive. All the tools and materials necessary to organize the allocation of work and direct its completion were set out neatly in upright trays. Even without looking at the forms, it was plain that work was being allocated and tasks communicated clearly, concisely and effectively. The telephone, a message pad and other necessary supervisory and sales tools were all set out for easy access.

The supervisor's working point was adjacent to the driveway and the workshop area, allowing him to immediately access the situation should an emergency arise or any problems occur with scheduled work. What struck me was that there would be many who would think that such a well defined level of control might be old-fashioned and even draconian. On the contrary, I am still a strong believer in the principle that the elements of control associated with supervision are very important and if you do not know what is happening, you cannot exercise those elements of control.

The very basic controlling principles of:-

(1) Assessing performance in terms of time, quantity, quality and sound work methods,

(2) Rejecting poor quality work and confirming standards,

(3) Disciplining promptly, objectively, constructively and briefly, are all the essence of sound work methods.

It appears clear to me that one of the major contributors to the success of this small business is the internalization of these principles and the various principles associated with directive leadership by the owner/operator. Certainly it was a pleasure to see someone who clearly enjoyed their work because they were well organized and able to manage their business confidently.

'But Dad, the licence says so'

Amusing but frightening tales seem to be coming my way thick and fast these days. I met with a gentleman recently on the subject of accreditation and he expressed some reservations about the meaningfulness of the various pieces of paper that organizations and individuals place upon the walls of their offices and reception areas.

This person's son recently obtained a driver's license. Feeling that manual gear change was really only as relevant as the Beta video cassette and five inch floppy disk drives, his son opted to be examined for and issued with a license to drive an automatic motor vehicle. It appears that he passed the automatic motor vehicle license test quite satisfactorily, but at the issuing point a clerical error was made and his license was endorsed to allow him to drive vehicles with manual gear change.

This small story in itself causes enough amusement and concern I am sure, but the really interesting part is the sting in the tail of the story. Apparently, this gentleman's son now believed that he should be able to step immediately into a manual gear change car and drive off. In fact, he asked his father for the use of the family four wheel drive (a manual) for the weekend and was quite shocked when his father flatly refused and said, 'You won't be driving anything other than an automatic while I have my way'.

'But Dad, the license says I can drive a manual'. This young man apparently genuinely believed that this clerical error had somehow miraculously achieved something that his driving instructor did not have on the agenda or the training program. Now we can only hope that our chances of encountering someone in a similar circumstance in our business dealings is as slim as there being one incorrectly licensed driver (if there is only one) in Australia. Whatever the odds, it is most important to remember that endorsement and competence do not always mean the same thing.

A number of senior managers have expressed the view that the awarding of a variety of certificates has done little, if anything, to improve the performance of their organization, despite their intention and expectation that the process would achieve exactly this end.

We all need to be aware that in the final analysis, we remain personally responsible for the standards achieved in our day to day work. Having received a certificate that says achieved, awarded, affiliated, recognized and so on is a past tense recognition of a process undertaken and completed. It is not a guarantee of future performance.

All organizations and their members need to view such important areas as quality of work and customer service as needing constant scrutiny. This monitoring process should be an essential part of maintaining the integrity of performance standards.

Constructive response will win the day

On one occasion, I wrote a Business Tip criticizing the administration of junior rowing. I was delighted to be approached by the senior administrators from the sport, who genuinely wanted to get as much information from me as possible, to incorporate into their plans for improvement.

In my view, this response to criticism is the only way to go. It is a clear reflection of an open minded and constructive attitude to the improvement of individual and group performance. One of the greatest difficulties we have in improving our own performance is keeping an open mind about constructive criticism. We speak about it so often as being essential to the development of a wide range of group activities, but how often do people practice what they preach?

Too many people throw the baby out with the bath water and adopt a totally defensive attitude. This is particularly unfortunate because it inhibits personal growth and future performance. So how can we ensure that we can get the benefit of constructive criticism without being defensive?

One of the first things that need to be included in our portfolio of skills is the ability to be objective. I believe that objectivity is very often directly proportional to a person's professionalism. Second, one has to retain the view that any person who is critical, does this with the clear intention of being helpful to the person or activity that they are criticizing. This is very difficult, but one has to retain the view that if a person takes the trouble to be critical, it is because they care and wish to see things change for the better.

Third, one has to truly believe the very old saying that: 'Nobody is perfect'. In the same vein, it follows that everybody is imperfect and will always be subject to criticism. Once you accept that this is a natural state, then criticism is something that you welcome and use as a tool to improve your performance. Unfortunately, these three principles sound great until you are the subject of the criticism. From there, the challenge is to have big shoulders upon which to rest that very open mind. Good luck! If you are able to achieve that objectivity, empathy and open-mindedness, you are destined to make big improvements in your performance.

End user focus important

In considering major road reconstruction near my office recently, it occurred to me again what a long trip it is from the drawing board to the real thing. Signs indicating exits were placed at the entrance to these exits, requiring luckless victims to cut across two lanes within one hundred meters to avoid missing the turn off (sound a bit complicated, it was). Merging lanes appeared out of nowhere like a visual illusion causing at best, hesitation and at worst, total confusion.

In these days of simulation by computer, it is likely that these various alterations were tested using computer models. Unfortunately, computers suffer no damage when their simulation has an accident and do not attract the attention to the problem that would occur in a real life simulation. This is not dissimilar to the experience of driving racing cars in an amusement arcade.

It never ceases to amaze me how professionals make the assumption that the users of the products would not be capable of providing useful input. This is most predominant in large scale projects where choice of supplier is very limited and often resources used are substantial, for example defence, roads, hospitals and so on.

At the other end of the spectrum, where consumer products are designed, a totally different approach is adopted by the extensive involvement of industrial designers, who are only too well aware of the heavy competition that occurs in the selection of consumer products from cars to electric appliances. The designers of large monopolistic industrial services need to acquire the end user focus which dominates activities in the consumer products area.

It is important to point out that the focus in dealing with the end user would not be on aesthetic issues, but on issues of functionality. If between them they could get 90% of the functional aspects correct, then perhaps they could go on and consider the aesthetic issues. In fact, this philosophy extends into the work situation even more dramatically. For many years organizations have spoken about worker participation, empowerment and quality circles with ever increasing concern about how to achieve a cooperative end result.

It is fascinating that both in the public arena and within organizations so much consultation appears to take place, but the parties directing the activities still suffer many frustrations because of an inability to access customers inside and outside the organization.

MBWA - alive, well and still effective

A senior manager in an organization consulted me recently on problems he felt were occurring because people at the coalface really did not have sufficient access to him. He attributed the access problem to particular supervisors and he was working on that problem but things were going just too slowly. He wanted my advice on how to get a quick fix to alleviate the problems associated with the lack of immediate access by both team members and supervisors to him.

Management by walking around', I said: 'It may be old, but it is still very effective'. Naturally, he knew about management by walking around (MBWA), having learned about it in theory and practiced it on previous assignments when he had worked in the consulting industry. On this occasion however, he was just so close to the problem that the very basics were not obvious to him.

So we had a lengthy discussion and revised the principles of management by walking around. I told him not to hesitate to get out there and have the closest possible look at what everybody was doing. 'Make sure that you approach this activity in a very supportive way', I said, 'and do not be seen as inspector or ogre from head office who is there to check on everybody'. 'Make it very clear that you are there to lend any support necessary to make sure the job is well done, but you still want to know in absolute detail what is going on, how the job is being done and exactly who is doing what.'

I was delighted when I received a call from the same manager some weeks later to tell me that MBWA was alive, well and still very effective. His management by walking around had an instant effect and totally brought the problem under control. So if you feel that you are not getting access to information you need in the management role you occupy, or in any job you do for that matter, or if you feel that people are not getting access to you when they should be, just apply some MBWA. It is very simple and very effective, but sometimes you just can't see the obvious solutions because they are so simple.

Management by walking around is like exercise, you have to do it on a regular basis to keep yourself totally trim and to keep your organization's activities trim as well. Get used to doing it regularly and you will find it refreshing for you and for the people who work with you. One of the main solutions to this particular problem is simple to state but not simple to implement. It is to listen, listen and then listen some more. The main problem is that most people are terrible listeners and even the listening that does take place is very superficial and the information does not get past the individual's defense mechanisms.

How do you know when you really have been listening? You will find that some of the things you are hearing are not what you want to hear. Try using this basic test and you will be getting a reasonable indication of your listening skills.

Conclusion

While the processes of implementing checking procedures in your work and the work of others are often physically simple, they are usually unexpectedly psychologically complex. This chapter has tried to reveal these issues and provide strategies to overcome the some of the many situations that can arise.

As always, it is what happens on the day that often determines the bigger picture in a way that top management policy cannot control. For this reason, *Goal Achievement Strategies* focuses on the day to day practical things that can be done to make sure the goals are achieved effectively and efficiently.

The notes below are a summary and reminder of the things that you can do to achieve your goals and help others achieve theirs.

Quality Control Checks

Check your own performance to achieve quality.

Adopt 'right first time' as your ideal.

CHECKING

- **Accept responsibility.**
- **Do the extra work.**
- **Know and apply the standard.**
- **Own the end result.**

Chapter Nine

Standardize

Introduction

To be truly effective and efficient you need to introduce standard procedures. Just as an elite athlete wins championships by making their basic skills second nature, outstanding work performance requires a commitment to planning, initiating, innovating and checking that becomes a standard procedure. In this chapter, this process is examined using a variety of anecdotes.

As emphasized throughout this book, the process is often physically simple, but the psychology of completing it and sticking to you standards is a challenge. The anecdotes aim to bring to life the psychological factors in a way that allows you to do the physical things with confidence and develop a personal philosophy that allows you to guide and motivate others.

Pride is good

I had the great pleasure the other day to visit the maintenance area of one of our major clients. This was extremely pleasurable for me because the supervisor in charge of the workshop clearly regarded the whole of the area with its various workshops and surrounding yards as his personal responsibility. This pride of ownership was clearly reflected in the condition of the various workshops. They were absolutely immaculate. This is all the more significant because these workshops were not for servicing computers, but involved the servicing of extremely heavy equipment with the associated substantial amounts of oil, grease and other fluids.

As I spoke to this particular person, I found myself wondering what it was that so impressed me about him as an individual. It dawned on me as he was leading me through the workshops to show me the systems that they used, that he was extremely proud of his work. He believed in the philosophy of 'right first time' and applied those principles consistently without exception. For this reason he was able to say with great pride, 'We don't have many comebacks here'.

The more we spoke, the more evident it became that there was a range of things that characterized this person as being special. He indicated quite happily that he brought in his own tools from home to do special jobs, because he saw no value in purchasing such specialist tools for jobs that occurred only once every three months.

Similarly, it became clear that the personal ownership of such tools was very similar to him to the acquisition of the specialist knowledge that made him capable of servicing such a wide range of equipment. He displayed a high level of enthusiasm about his work and about the reputation that he and his employer enjoyed in their industry. He did not hesitate to say that he enjoyed his work tremendously and was totally committed to first class results, both technically and financially.

Reflecting on this conversation some time later, it was clear to me that the success this particular client enjoys is directly attributable to its capacity to select individuals with that sense of pride in their work. In addition, this was complemented by the client's willingness to give these outstanding people the opportunity to perform in a way that they can be proud of.

This match of an individual with pride in his/her ability to achieve with an employer who recognizes the individual's need to achieve brought about an almost magical result. I was delighted to have the opportunity to observe the outcome.

The moral of this story is that people with a sense of pride in their work and a need to achieve do exist and employers with a commitment to people of this type also exist. The two, when they get together, can produce great results, but one without the other can result in a situation of total frustration and total lack of performance.

So, if you are an employee with pride and commitment, find yourself an employer who is keen to nurture that type of behavior. Similarly, if you are an employer looking for that type of employee, just take heart, they do exist and they are well worth waiting for.

Profit without injury

It was most refreshing to have a lengthy conversation recently with a high flying manager from one the country's most successful organizations. He happened to raise an issue with one of my favorite 'hobby horses' - the questioning of Total Quality Management (TQM) and other acronyms.

This executive put forward very strongly a convincing argument for the successful management of companies without the frills associated with the latest management theories. What impressed me most was this very hard driving and very profit-oriented executive's strong belief that the absolute personal safety of workers was the most critical factor for an organization's success.

He was adamant that there was never, never, never any excuse for personal injury to workers because safe working practices were an integral part of efficient working practices. If only some of the world's largest enterprises could embrace this view was all I could think as he presented his argument for this commitment to safety.

In pursuing his argument, he was most fired up about the fact that Total Quality Management (TQM) and other gimmicks (as he described them) provided a cop-out option for managers who lacked the general management skill to bring together the right team to combine effective marketing with operational efficiency and deliver a profit to the shareholders. Personally, I was inspired by this rare moment of expansiveness from this individual. I knew from experience within the organizations where he had worked that he was highly regarded as a tough but fair, no bull dust operator. It had been explained to me by his colleagues how he had acquired a reputation for increasing the personal net worth of both shareholders and employees without a major fuss.

Are we looking for the promised land while the farm under our feet sprouts weeds as a result of our neglect and lack of skill? I think there is certainly a strong indication that many managers are having trouble following the plot and are happy to follow any new scheme for potential salvation. Worse still, I believe many of these schemes have become 'institutionalized', feeding off their own swarm of flies that have gathered around the smell of a good feed. Up until now, the only spanner in the works has been the victims thrown out on the piles of retrenched workers littering the corporate streets. However, there seems to be something of a new order amongst those rising in more successful companies. This new order has the confidence in their own abilities and are not scared to say that success can be achieved simply if one is prepared to take personal responsibility. In the corporate world, profit is the goal and people are the soul. Managers who understand and accept this value will succeed in the long term and build a better corporate world for the community. Certainly, there have been sufficient examples of how not to do it, but to undermine managers' confidence in themselves, and their willingness to commit to personal responsibility, is not the answer to creating a new long term successful order. Building of personal value and respect for others as espoused by my high flying companion certainly has my support and I would recommend it as a sound business strategy.

Effort versus results

Over the years, I have had numerous opportunities to assess my employees accurately by virtue of the results that they achieve. This has really confirmed in my mind my long standing view that appearance of activity is totally unrelated to actual results. One employee whom I recall vividly, worked virtually the minimum prescribed hours. When he was at work, however, he did nothing but work and when he worked, he worked to 100% of his capacity.

Strangely, the ability to work to 100% of capacity is very rare. Needless to say, the individual that works in this way achieves the same outstanding results as my very memorable employee. The key factor in being successful is to: **determine very clearly what bring results and work with that formula to make the best use of your time.**

It is a fact that we all fall into habit patterns, whether they are good or bad, and developing good habit patterns is just a matter of hard work, setting small and then larger goals for change, and sticking to what we resolve. Of course, there are numerous distractions for any course of change but in this area, being successful comes back to you and the questions of motivation, resolve, effort versus results. All of these things rest with the individual - you.

I have had the opportunity to work with a variety of highly successful entrepreneurs over time and it has become clear to me that their success is attributable to a very large extent to their internal obsession or drive to perform at the highest level. Certainly, they had other factors that affected just how successful they were, but universally, they have had an inner drive which seems to be beyond their control. Very often, this drive can be traced back to an event or events which started them on the road to proving their worth to themselves and to others.

If you do not have this inner drive, then being successful means creating an environment or situation where the level of drive you do have is expanded, exaggerated, developed, or whatever word is most comfortable for you. In this way you create the environment where you can achieve at the level that you have set for yourself.

I have always said that discontent occurs mostly from the equation 'effort equals results', getting out of balance. A huge effort with little result brings discontent. I should point out that there is a distinct difference between economy of effort and little effort. Economy of effort, as discussed in relation to working 100% for 100% of the time, is your goal. Success through lack of effort is a different circumstance. Traditionally, the formula 'effort equals results' is normally a fairly stable one with both sides of the equation being relatively equal. It is well worth keeping this in mind if you do have to develop artificial motivators to get you up to that obsession level of effort consistent with entrepreneurial success.

Careful use of resources

There has been a lot of talk in business about efficiency and effectiveness for a very long time going back to the original time and motion studies of the 20th Century. These two characteristics of efficiency and effectiveness are very important for day to day activities in all our lives.

Efficiency is all about making the best possible use of our resources without waste. Effectiveness is about applying our resources to get the best possible outcome with the tools we have available.

This situation is very beautifully illustrated by the expression of the 24-egg omelet. This expression is usually used to describe the person who can make a delicious omelet, but uses two dozen eggs in the process. Such a person is highly effective in making a delicious omelet but terribly inefficient in the use of resources. At the other end of the scale is the person who makes omelets that will feed twice as many people, but waters down the egg to achieve the result. This demonstrates a great use of resources, but not very effective in satisfying the customer. The person who is both efficient and effective uses milk to make the omelet in just the right proportion to make a delicious omelet but makes the eggs go the maximum possible distance.

All of us are faced with the challenge of efficiency and effectiveness every day. The person who will be highly successful is the one is able to balance the quality of the final product with the need to make maximum use of the resources. Be careful not to be literal and try to explain away this example by the skill of the chef or the quality of the raw materials. The aim is to appreciate that all situations provide you with resources. They may be physical, financial, human, psychological, philosophical or impossible to explain, but it is you view and use of them that determines your success.

Think carefully about that you want. Look around you to see what resources you have and then review that goal. Next you plan, initiate, innovate, check and then standardize to make the effort vs results equation work as much in you favor as you can –every time. Good luck.

Bureaucracy - doing business with yourself

There is a very old story told about the British Navy. After World War I, the Navy apparently had a large fleet of ships, a large contingent of sailors and officers and a very small administration group. Without a war to fight, the focus changed and by the time World War II rolled around the Navy had very few ships, few sailors and officers and a gigantic administrative support organization.

How does this happen? One of the problems associated with having a large work organization, is the obsession that develops with making sure that everything appears to be efficient, effective and fair. I will emphasize the 'appears to be' because appearances far outstrip reality in this regard. A classic example of this type of activity, which can be found in both private and public enterprises, occurs when individuals who have worked for organizations for many years are asked to apply in detail for any new vacancy.

Recently, a senior public servant lamented to me the need for him to supply his entire life and work history for consideration by a promotions board when he had been employed by the organization for over fifteen years. The standard line of response to criticism of this strategy is 'Requiring every candidate, regardless of their origin, to apply on equal terms is the only basis upon which a fair decision can be made.' It is difficult to argue with this proposition. In reality, however, it is an example of complete abandonment of management responsibility.

The individuals who support this particular philosophy are saying, 'I am not prepared to take responsibility for the effectiveness of my management decisions and I will do everything possible to ensure that people think I gave everyone an even chance'.

In fact, presentation of all the resumes from all candidates in no way improves the effectiveness of the decision because there is no guarantee that the information will be used anyway. Nevertheless, because the process <u>appears</u> fair, criticism of management is much less likely. Unfortunately this and numerous other examples relating to the letting of contracts, the reclassification of positions, internal transfer of resources, and so on ensure that bureaucracies spend a large percentage of their time doing business with themselves.

The key fault that brings about this bureaucratic behavior, is the inability of senior managers in bureaucracies to implement true people management. Two factors are major contributors to senior management's failure to successfully manage people. The first is an inability to differentiate the capable from the incompetent and the second is the unwillingness to act because of the fear of making errors in relation to management appointments.

So how do you prevent this horrible thing called bureaucracy from existing in a large organization? It is possible and has been achieved by a number of significant public companies in Australia, placing them at the head of the list of well managed and profitable companies. The strategy they use is very simple. The company allocates responsibility for management of expenditure and revenue to the lowest appropriate point in the structure. Reporting is based on the financial results achieved at that level and assessment and supervision of those results normally requires no more than two levels of management before reporting to the board of directors of the organization.

So the business tip for fighting the dreaded bureaucratic plague is to make people accountable and do not set up layers upon layers of people to check on the people who actually do the work. Interestingly, this process of 'flattening the enterprise' is not new it just does not get done effectively because the basic system of trust in allowing team members to do their checking is never applied.

Balance the load

I was conducting a Personal and Management Effectiveness Program for a group of real estate agents recently. It was interesting to note that one of these proprietors, who had been identified as extremely successful, attributed his success to working extremely hard, but pointed out that he had a mini burnout every six weeks. To counteract this burnout effect, every six weeks he would take at least four days holiday to recharge his batteries. Thus, he had a short period of high activity that he was able to maintain on a cyclical basis because he standardized his work routine.

Almost immediately after this, I had the opportunity to do a joint presentation to another group with a colleague I have known for many years. She is respected as being successful in the very demanding personnel consulting area. Regrettably, over many years, she still has not taken a holiday longer than seven days and even this short break is taken no more than once a year. This is despite the fact that she is employed by a corporation and has substantial accumulated recreation leave.

The term recreation means to re-create. If you do not re-create, you will deteriorate.

The clue to getting the balance in this very important area of work and play is to listen to the messages your body and mind sends you. If you are prone to minor illnesses, irritable a good deal of the time and more inclined to make mistakes, it may well be time to consider when you last had a proper holiday.

There are also things you can do on a day-to-day basis to maintain the balance. I recommend to many groups that a 30 minute relaxation session four times per week can be very helpful to prevent an unhealthy buildup of stress.

Just take the time to find a quiet location, lie down and try to clear your mind of negative thoughts by concentrating on images that make you feel relaxed and positive. A favorite of mine is to imagine that I am lying on the beach in the late afternoon with the sun at a very low ebb, and that I am quietly dosing off. What I try to do is imagine the feeling of the gentle cool breeze, very slight warmth of the sun and that overall lazy, hazy feeling.

People's ability to do relaxation exercises varies considerably. It is a good idea to determine your individual ability to relax and then take appropriate action to help yourself reach an appropriate level of relaxation. You may need to attend a relaxation group. You may be one of those people who get sufficient information out of a suitable book on healthy life styles. If you are lucky you may need to do nothing more than what I have suggested to you in the above paragraph. Whatever the strategy is for you, the most important thing is that you do something to balance your lifestyle.

Standardizing you goal achievement activities should not be about working non-stop.

Conclusion

The key to successful use of the principle of using standard methods to get the best levels of efficiency and effectiveness is to remember that it is part of bringing the whole goal achievement Psychoframe together.

- Standardise your methods to maximise efficiency.

STANDARDISE

- **Copy the best.**
- **Speed it up, shorten it, organise it better.**
- **Document the best system.**
- **Be the best.**

Time for some personal reflection before you proceed to the concluding chapter.

Most importantly, what can you do to achieve your goals?

Chapter Ten

Conclusion

As I have stressed throughout the book, this is just a few ideas that I hope will contribute in some way to your life journey by helping you focus on what you want and how to get there.

In contrast to *Goal Achievement Strategies*, many books have been written that tell inspirational stories of what others have achieved. These can be interesting and inspiring, but they are always about someone else's journey. This book is about your journey and I have tried to use case studies that show how most of lives are 'ordinary' but the opportunity always exists to make the most of this ordinary life.

In the Annex I have provided a 'clean' copy of the GRF and GAQ for you to copy and use as often as you like. In addition, the answers are provided again (with a bit of variation to emphasise that there are many right answers).

I hope you found the process fun as well as useful. The goal was to keep it focused on you and what you want from life. Unfortunately, some of us never have the opportunity to even think about that, let alone do something about it, because circumstances really do restrict our options. For most people, however, there is some room to move.

The first key point of *Goal Achievement Strategies* is that how you approach the room you have to move can make a big difference to the outcome you get. The second is that it is not just about enthusiasm and an irrepressible nature, although that can help, it is about being organised, getting on with the job, realising you can innovate, taking personal responsibility and being systematic.

The third key point is that this is your life and you have to choose how to live it. Having done so, your goal is to accept who you are and be happy about it.

ANNEX

Goal Review Form (GRF)

Name: _____

Date: _____

1.   Currently, success to me means

_____

_____

_____

2.   Rate where are you now with respect to this current goal by marking an X along the Scale of Success to indicate your current progress.

Scale of Success

0   20   40   60   80   100%
Just Starting   Where I want to be

3.   Strategies for the achievement of my success goals

ACTION   BY WHEN

_____

_____

_____

_____

_____

_____

GOAL ACHIEVEMENT QUESTIONNAIRE (GAQ)

Name: _____ Date:_____

INSTRUCTIONS

The Goal Achievement Questionnaire (GAQ) is designed to help you learn more about your approach to managing personal challenges. It is open-ended and requires written answers.

The questionnaire contains a series of statements followed by a space for you to write your response. You are required to respond as if you were speaking to someone who may make a statement or ask a question. Your response should be about your own attitudes, beliefs and experiences. You should not respond with a question.

Do not worry if you have no experience in this area. The questionnaire uses no special jargon or other expressions which would be unfamiliar to you. Alternatively, although the questions are intended to be general, you may feel happier answering in relation to a particular situation you have experienced. Feel free to use any method of approach. The aim is to allow you to give your views on a variety of issues by simulating a discussion.

HERE IS A SAMPLE OF WHAT YOU WILL BE REQUIRED TO DO

Statement: Can Goal Achievement be learned?

Response: Of course, it is a skill.

You may write as much as you like in the space provided, but you need to make only two different points to complete the item and achieve the maximum score.

The questionnaire is completed with a time limit because the situations which are simulated are usually done under pressure with no opportunity to correct errors made.

You will have 30 minutes to do as many of the questions as possible. Work quickly but not so fast that you make mistakes. Ask any questions before you begin.

PLEASE TURN OVER AND START WORK

GOAL ACHIEVEMENT QUESTIONNAIRE

1.   Statement: What is the value of personal goal setting?

      Response:

_____

_____

2.   Statement: What does it mean to be a self-starter?

      Response:

_____

_____

3.   Statement: How can everybody be innovative?

      Response:

_____

_____

4.   Statement: How do I know if I have done a quality job?

      Response:

_____

_____

5.   Statement: What is personal efficiency?

      Response:

_____

_____

6.   Statement: How do I use goal setting to motivate myself?

Response:

_____

_____

7.   Statement: Shouldn't I wait for someone else to show me the way?

Response:

_____

_____

8.   Statement: Why should I always look for a better way of doing things?

Response:

_____

_____

9.   Statement: Getting it right the first time seems pretty unrealistic to me.
Response:

_____

_____

10.   Statement: Developing systems just seems to slow things down.
Response:

_____

_____

11.   Statement: What is the value of planning?

Response:

_____

_____

12.   Statement: Won't people be threatened by me taking the initiative?

Response:

_____

_____

13.   Statement: All the best ways of doing things should have been thought of already.

Response:

_____

_____

14.   Statement: Everybody makes mistakes!

Response:

_____

_____

15.   Statement: What is the value of developing standard work systems?

Response:

_____

_____

16.   Statement: I could be getting things done with the time that I would waste planning.

Response:

_____

_____

17.   Statement: I just can't seem to get started on things.

Response:

_____

_____

18.   Statement: How do I innovate?

Response:

_____

_____

19.   Statement: Isn't it better to have someone else check what you do?

Response:

_____

_____

20.   Statement: What is personal effectiveness?

Response:

_____

_____

21.   Statement: How far ahead should I plan?

Response:

_____

_____

22.   Statement: What's the value of having initiative?

Response:

_____

_____

23.   Statement: Won't people be threatened by me always trying to find a better way?

Response:

_____

_____

24.   Statement: I can't always get it right.

Response:

_____

_____

25.   I'm just not the type of person who gets organised!

Response:

_____

_____

CHECK YOUR ANSWERS IF YOU HAVE TIME

GOAL ACHIEVEMENT ANSWERS

1. What is the value of personal goal setting?

- Motivation
- Clarity of purpose
- Allows assessment

2. What does it mean to be a self-starter?

- To not need others' supervision
- Have energy/drive/motivation
- Have self-confidence

3. How can everybody be innovative?

- Changing for the better
- Using creative thinking
- Looking for continual improvements
- Be inventive/imaginative
- By looking forward

4. How do I know if I have done a quality job?

- Meets the standards
- Product is functional

5. What is personal efficiency?

- Using the least resources necessary
- Getting the optimal result by organising materials

6. How do I use goal setting to motivate myself?

- Think of achievement/satisfaction upon reaching goal
- Set realistic goals
- Set a goal you desire and work towards it.

7. Shouldn't I wait for someone else to show me the way?

- No
- Increased drive if own plan
- Self determination of plan

8. Why should I always look for a better way of doing things.

- Efficiency
- Continual improvement is possible

9. Getting it right the first time seems pretty unrealistic to me.

- No
- Not if you check your work

10. Developing systems just seems to slow things down.

- No
- Actually working to a plan is quicker

11. What is the value of planning?

- Best allocation of resources
- Strategy for implementation

12. Won't people be threatened by me taking the initiative?

- Something you do for you
- Self development
- Allow consideration

13. All the best ways of doing things should have been thought of already.

- No
- Individuality
- Improvements/advancements

14. Everybody makes mistakes!

- Probably yes
- Learning occurs
- Grow from experiences

15. What is the value of developing standard work systems?

- Allows delegation
- Develops efficiency
- You can work to a plan

16. I could be getting things done with the time that I would waste planning.

- Expression of disagreement
- Statement regarding value of planning

17. I just can't seem to get started on things.

- Just do it
- Find something to motivate you
- With practice it will become easier

18. How do I innovate?

- Look for improvements
- Use goals/brainstorming or planning
- Be creative

19. Isn't it better to have someonelse check what you do?

- No
- Efficiency
- Increases self worth or self confidence

20. What is personal effectiveness?

- Successful completion
- Personally being able to do a task

21. How far ahead should I plan?

- As necessary for achievement
- For meaningful length of time

22. What's the value of having initiative?

- Motivation
- Success

23. Won't people be threatened by me always trying to find a better way?

- It's for self development
- Something done for you

24. I can't always get it right.

- Practice
- Learn from mistakes
- Check work

25. I'm just not the type of person who gets organised!

- Practice
- Organization is a learned skill
- You can be what you want
- Do a little bit at a time

INDEX

Other titles and media

Other books and audio materials by Karel de Laat include Hints for Personal Success, Business Tips, Practical Management Strategies, Career Management Strategies, Sales and Customer Service Strategies and Personal Success Strategies.

Further Reading

Unless otherwise credited, the quotes by in this book are from *Elbert Hubbard's Scrap Book.*[6]

[1] Opie, I & P (eds), *The Oxford Dictionary of Nursery Rhymes*, Oxford University Press, London, 1951, pp. 296-7.

[2] There are many books and audio programs on the subject of relaxation and visualization. I recommend selecting one that suits your needs in terms of how, where and when you want to apply the techniques and give preference to one that is authored by a registered counselor or psychologist aligned with a reputable organization.

[3] AM Colman (ed), *A Dictionary of Psychology*, Oxford University Press, Oxford, 2009, p. 607.

[4] Karel de Laat, *Personal Success Strategies*, de Laat & Co, Brisbane, 2015.

[5] C Duhigg, *The Power of Habit*, Random House, New York, 2012.

[6] E Hubbard, *Elbert Hubbard's Scrap Book*, Wise & Co, New York City, 1923.

www.ingramcontent.com/pod-product-compliance
Lightning Source LLC
Chambersburg PA
CBHW071542040426
42452CB00008B/1091